bite to eat place

bite to eat place:
an anthology of contemporary food
poetry and poetic prose

editors:

Andrea Adolph

Donald L. Vallis

Anne F. Walker

REDWOOD COAST PRESS

Library of Congress Catalog Card Number: 95 - 67899
bite to eat place

ISBN 0-9640933-1-6
Poetry
I. Adolph, Andrea, 1965— II. Vallis, Donald L., 1963—
III. Walker, Anne F., 1964—

Typesetting, cover photo and design: Donald L. Vallis

Redwood Coast Press
Box 9552, Oakland, CA 94613
in Canada:
Box 377, Stn. P. Toronto, Ontario, M5S 2S9

Printed in the United States on recycled, acid-free paper with soy-
based inks.

TABLE OF CONTENTS:

for Jamil

Michael Ondaatje

The Cinnamon Peeler

If I were a cinnamon peeler
I would ride your bed
and leave the yellow bark dust
on your pillow.

Your breasts and shoulders would reek
you could never walk through markets
without the profession of my fingers
floating over you. The blind would
stumble certain of whom they approached
though you might bathe
under rain gutters, monsoon.

Here on the upper thigh
at this smooth pasture
neighbour to your hair
or the crease
that cuts your back. This ankle.
You will be known among strangers
as the cinnamon peeler's wife.

I could hardly glance at you
before marriage
never touch you
—your keen nosed mother, your rough brothers.
I buried my hands
in saffron, disguised them
over smoking tar,
helped the honey gatherers . . .

When we swam once
I touched you in water
and our bodies remained free,
you could hold me and be blind of smell.
You climbed the bank and said

       this is how you touch other women
the grass cutter's wife, the lime burner's daughter.
And you searched your arms
for the missing perfume
           and knew

     what good is it
to be the lime burner's daughter
left with no trace
as if not spoken to in the act of love
as if wounded without the pleasure of a scar.

You touched
your belly to my hands
in the dry air and said
I am the cinnamon
peeler's wife. Smell me.

Deborah Artman

Nanny from Maroon Town

Nanny from Maroon Town never heard of me. She's skinny like a man. She's walking and crushing ideas with her feet. She's selling fruit to tourists from a basket. She's crooning to them in Padua and calling them nasty names.

Nanny from Maroon Town knows what heat is. She moves slow and talks loud at night. I can hear her out my window. Her laugh is big and strange like a strong smell. I am smelling my skin to see what my smell is, what I might smell like to someone else who might have grown fond of my smell.

Nanny is skinny because she doesn't need to eat. She hardly sleeps either, maybe she'll lean against a tree and rest. She knows her fruit in the dark, knows how they feel, their shape. Who knows what she's wishing. She leans over babies and strokes their cheeks. She mesmerizes them. She swears softly and they bubble back at her. She could steal them if she wanted but she just sucks them up, looks away, never thinking about food, never thinking about the water, the thin place where the sun falls in, swallowing.

Chana Bloch

Eating Babies

1

FAT
is the soul of this flesh.
Eat with your hands, slow, you will understand
breasts, why everyone
adores them—Rubens' great custard nudes—why
we can't help sleeping with
pillows.

The old woman in the park pointed,
Is it yours?
Her gold eye-teeth gleamed.

I bend down, taste the fluted
nipples, the elbows, the pads
of the feet. Nibble earlobes, dip
my tongue in the salt fold
of shoulder and throat.

Even now he is changing,
as if I were
licking him thin.

2

HE SQUEEZES his eyes tight
to hide
and blink! he's still here.
It's always a surprise.

Safety-fat,
angel-fat,

steal it in mouthfuls,
store it away
where you save

the face that you touched
for the last time
over and over,
your eyes closed

so it wouldn't go away.

3

WATCH HIM sleeping. Touch
the pulse where
the bones haven't locked
in his damp hair:
the navel of dreams.
His eyes open for a moment, underwater.

His arms drift in the dark
as your breath
washes over him.

Bite one cheek. Again.
It's your own
life you lean over, greedy,
going back for more.

Lorna Crozier

Learning to Read

Mary is reading recipes:
cinnamon she says again and again,
then sprinkles some from the can
on her fingertips, holds them
to her nose, licks them clean.
This is what she knew before,
the taste and smell, but now
there's this, *cinnamon*
written in her mother's hand
on the index card and *1 tsp.*

Surely here is the story of a life,
the recipes making her see
her mother's hands
sticky with pastry, red from beets,
smelling of vinegar and garlic
or apples and peach.

She has saved this box
since her mother's death
and opened it at night,
her husband and the kids in bed.
For years she ran her fingers
over a buttersmudge, a smear of
molasses that dripped from a spoon.
These she could read,
but now the words!

And it's as if her mother were here
again beside her in the kitchen

measuring *cinnamon*,
that most beautiful of sounds,
while Mary reads out loud
what is needed next
and finds it
newly labeled on the shelf.

Claire Harris

Child This is the Gospel on Bakes

First   strain sunlight through avocado leaves
then pour into a dim country kitchen through bare
windows   on a wooden table freshly scrubbed
'I'm warning you   a lazy person is a nasty
person'   flurry of elbows
place a yellow oil cloth   on this   a bowl
a kneading board   a dull knife   spoons
then draw up an old chair with a cane seat   on
the back of the chair have a grandfather carve flowers
birds   the child likes to trace sweep of petals
curve of wings   to tease a finger along
edges softened by age   and numberless polishings
The initiate kneels on the seat
afterwards there will be a pattern of cane left
on her knees to trace
around her neck like a cape tie the huge blue apron
so that only her head and thin bare arms are visible
Place a five pound milk can painted green
with yellow trim and full of flour
a tall salt jar   salt clumping together
fresh grated nutmeg   sugar in a green can
butter in a clay cooler   a red enamelled
cup brimming with cold water
Have someone say 'be careful now
don't make a mess'
The child takes one handful of flour   makes a hill
outside a humming bird whirrs   sun gleams
on her hill   she adds another handful   another and another
she makes a careful mountain   then lightly walks
her fingers to the top   she flattens the crest   an old

voice in her ear   *'don't you go making yourself out*
special now'   she watches as flour sifts down
sides of her mountain   then scoops out a satisfactory
hollow   she can see humming birds at red
hibiscus   beyond a small boy   barefeet
on the plum tree his voice shrilling king
of the mountain threats   old voice eggs him on
Into the hollow   daughter   put a pinch of salt   a
a little sugar for each handful of flour
as much butter as can be held in a nutshell
'Ready' she calls   waits
Even if she looks straight ahead she still sees
from the corner of her eye   lamps their bowls full
gathering sunlight   the way girls should
waiting patiently for evening
Behind her there is always someone preparing pastry
on a grey marble-topped table
the rolling pin presses dough   thinner
and thinner towards the round edge
the maker pushing pastry
to transparency
ices the pin folds the pastry over butter
begins again   then finally the last stretching roll
till it seems skin must break into a ragged O
She is rigid with apprehension   this is something
to do with her
so she does not hear the voice over her shoulder say
'drizzle this baking powder all over'
handing her a spoon   until she is tapped lightly
starts to the chorus 'this child always dreaming yes
but what you going to do with her'
Her mother saying ever so carefully 'let her dream
while she can'   she begins to knead
butter into the flour   her mother sprinkles grated lemon
peel   and when she has crumbs she makes another hollow

adds water while someone clucks warnings
she begins to knead the whole together
not forgetting the recurring dream in which she climbs
through a forest of leaves she kneads   stepping
bravely from branch to branch   miles above ground
she kneads and kneads trying to make it smooth
she finds a bird that talks
and flies away just as she is beginning
to understand   she kneads   and finally someone says
'that's good enough' she kneads just a little more
she is watching the bird   which is flying
straight into the sun
where it lives bravely
a rum bottle full of water is thrust into her hands
which she must wash again   then flour the bottle
to roll out her dough which she has made into a ball
outside the high-pitched yelling of small boys at cricket
she is better at cricket than at bakes
she will never be as good at bakes as her mother is
or her aunt   or her great aunt   or her grandmother
or even the kitchen maid who is smiling openly
because the child's bakes are not round
her mother says gently 'I'll show you a trick'
she rolls the dough out for her again   takes a glass
cuts out perfect rounds of bakes
together they lay them out on a baking sheet
we'll decorate yours with a fork   dad will be proud
together they cover her bakes with wet cloth
when the oven is ready her mother will test the heat
sprinkling water on a tin sheet

Andrea Adolph

Someone Had to Eat It

1
In the seventies women shared food
like secrets, crocks filled with sourdough,
with brandied fruit set fire
on special occasions. Secrets
passed on to me, my mother and her rice
diets, her juice fasts, her face
lifted to whittle away at fifteen years of marriage.
I dressed up in her habits. Lunch at school was
orange juice and a proud announcement of denial.
My fifth grade teacher thought it some religion. But then,
home and the freezer to face, a large yellow
bowl of experiments. Single,
my mother had taken up baking.

2
In high school I could bench press
ninety pounds. But that was before strength
was a virtue, before I knew
where it comes from. Thin girls didn't press anything
and were beautiful in their prom dresses,
tulle and taffeta easy over their hipless
hips. I ate three days a week and still had arms
that were legacies of German women whose bodies
were purposeful, like cotton underwear or thick-
soled walking shoes.

3
I vomited in private
cubicles

in public restrooms, learned
quickly to walk out white-faced,
eyes round, an apologetic hand
to the stomach. Even now it sounds good
as the nausea returns, as I recall the day
after my mother's wake, the house purged
of relatives, the bright pink bundt cake confettied
so much like a party no one had the heart
to eat it.

Vidas Gvozdzius

Pig Roast

My father places hot smooth stones
in the pig's throat and belly, wraps
the pig tight in chicken wire, sewn
metal cutting deep into the flesh.
He lowers it into a hole weaved
with baked bricks and thick banana leaves.

My twelve year old sister skips
among her aunts. Already she tries
on their gestures, watching the men
from the corner of her eyes.
Uncle Milan enters through the back
gate, still unwashed from the dirt
of the mills. He strips off his shirt,
sweat streaking diagonals across
his chest. We drink, speak about the coming
lay-offs; about the farms and small towns
our parents left; the 1961 Yankees.

Hours later, the pig's ears are sliced
for soup. Father wraps the pig,
gentle, honoring its flesh and our
hunger. We eat the meat with rice,
warm beans, and watermelon.

The silence of full bellies comes upon us.
At the edge of the quiet, a twilight
whistle blows, calling men to the darkness.

Sheila Meads

Leftovers

I smells funny, doesn't it? But what is it that it reminds her of? ...something ...something ...ahh ...Easter, that's it. Easter ham... Easter roasting red pig, glistening, sword-hilt cloves jutting from criss-cross furrows of brown sizzling fat and underneath... underneath—sweet sweet painfully pink flesh

Easter at the in-laws.

From her beside herself place, Angie watches Angie take her hand from the element and turn the dial right down, calm as anything, calm as turning down the roast because, oh, by the way, Hon, company's going to be a bit late. She's mildly interested from her beside herself place to see the three perfect red half-rings turning white on her pretty hand where Ken placed his gold ring ...his kisses ...his own hand, browner, harder, larger only two years ago...

And there was that mark, wasn't there? The bumpy one right at the base of his thumb that Angie used to run her fingers over when they were watching T.V. together. Skewered and scarred from an errant nail when he was eleven. She loved that hand.

Funny that she should be able to see *that* so clearly now when she couldn't for the life of her remember what his smile was like...

Angie waits for the pain to come, watching serenely from her beside herself place. She can almost see it slide down her arm, curling under her wrist, winding up and around her palm, through three fingers, three times, round and round and round 'til there's nowhere left to go but *up* and when it does, she's actually surprised because up it comes fast as a viper, bright as a sun-faced viper, *so bright it makes her gasp out loud!* ...gasp the way she's wanted to but couldn't from her beside herself place all this time since the funeral, since they said the prayers, swaying with the trees over the shiny mahogany casket and she was positive they were all wrong, that he wasn't the right size or shape for that rough grassy cut-out. But they sprinkled the dirt on top of him anyway, blackish-brown and bittersweet like Oreo cookie crumbs and then drank tea and ate quartered salmon and egg sandwiches in her newly papered kitchen while his red-nosed-eyes-streaming mother stood wringing her handkerchief in the corner.

And there was the ham too, wasn't there? On soft white bread, cold and sliced thin with only a dab of mustard. The smell of it with strong coffee perking in the background—just like Easter Monday. Just like it was all over.

And really, didn't they all say what a trooper she was? Handling it so well. Going back to work right after. Getting on with things...

Angie swallows that viper, puts her whole screaming fist into her mouth and chokes it down so that now she can finally gasp and gulp and fall to the floor blubbering, basting the cold white linoleum with the truth of the matter, because the truth is she's just beside herself with grief.

Scott Minar

Gumbo

See child, there's 'crow
in the mud, mustard and my daddy's
ghost, oh yes, and sometime
they ain't no wind to call it. I ride
down in the flat
till I see lillies smilin'
like they got teeth,
an' in a while the pond open
to the river. You see snakes down there
like okra floatin' in a pot,
an' I beat 'em with the pole
but they almost get in anyway.
An' one night, the moon yella
as a turnip an' squirrels floppin'
in the trees like they's monkees,
I seen it, skin fallin' off
like you cooked a pig's head
too long an' felt sorry
for the po' thing,
I swear to God.

bpNichol

The Mouth

1.

You were never supposed to talk when it was full. It was better to keep it shut if you had nothing to say. You were never supposed to shoot it off. It was better to be seen than heard. It got washed out with soap if you talked dirty. You were never supposed to mouth-off, give them any of your lip, turn up your nose at them, give them a dirty look, an evil eye or a baleful stare. So your mouth just sat there, in the middle of your still face, one more set of muscles trying not to give too much away. 'Hey! SMILE! what's the matter with you anyway?'

2.

Probably there are all sorts of stories. Probably my mouth figures in all sorts of stories when I was little but I don't remember any of them. I don't remember any stories about my mouth but I remember it was there. I remember it was there and I talked & sang & ate & used it all the time. I don't remember anything about it but the mouth remembers. The mouth remembers what the brain can't quite wrap its tongue around & that's what my life's become. My life's become my mouth's remembering, telling stories with the brain's tongue.

3.

I must have been nine. I'm pretty sure I was nine because I remember I was the new boy in school. I remember I was walking on my way there, the back way, thru the woods, & here was this kid walking towards me, George was his name, & I said 'hi George & he said 'I don't like your mouth' & grabbed me & smashed my face into his knee. It was my first encounter with body art or it was my first encounter with someone else's idea of cosmetic surgery. It was translation or composition. He rearranged me.

4.

The first dentist called me the Cavity Kid & put 35 fillings into me. The second dentist said the first dentist was a charlatan, that all the fillings had fallen out, & put 38 more fillings in me. The third dentist had the shakes from his years in the prisoner of war camp & called me his 'juicy one', saliva frothing from my mouth as his shakey hand approached me. The fourth dentist never looked at me. His nurse put me out with the sleeping gas & then he'd enter the room & fill me. The fifth dentist said my teeth were okay but my gums would have to go, he'd have to cut me. The sixth dentist said well he figured an operation on the foot was okay coz the foot was a long way away but the mouth was just a little close to where he thot he lived & boy did we ever agree because I'd begun to see that every time I thot of dentists I ended the sentence with the word 'me'. My mouth was me. I wasn't any ancient Egyptian who believed his Ka was in his nose – nosiree – I was just a Kanadian kid & had my heart in my mouth every time a dentist approached me.

5.

It all begins with the mouth. I shouted waaa when I was born, maaa when I could name her, took her nipple in, the rubber nipple of the bottle later, the silver spoon, mashed peas, dirt, ants, anything with flavour I could shove there, took the tongue & flung it 'round the mouth making sounds, words, sentences, tried to say the things that made it possible to reach him, kiss her, get my tongue from my mouth into some other. I liked that, liked the fact the tongue could move in mouths other than its own, & that so many things began there – words did, meals, sex – & tho later you travelled down the body, below the belt, up there you could belt out a duet, share a belt of whiskey, undo your belts & put your mouths together. And I like the fact that we are rhymed, mouth to mouth, & that it begins here, on the tongue, in the pun, comes from mouth her mouth where we all come from.

6.

I always said I was part of the oral tradition. I always said poetry was an oral art. When I went into therapy my therapist always said I had an oral personality. I got fixated on oral sex, oral gratification & notating the oral reality of the poem. At the age of five when Al Watts Jr was still my friend I actually said, when asked who could do something or other, 'me or Al' & only years later realized how the truth's flung out of you at certain points & runs on ahead. And here I've been for years running after me, trying to catch up, shouting 'it's the oral', 'it all depends on the oral', everybody looking at my bibliography, the too many books & pamphlets, saying with painful accuracy: 'that bp – he really runs off at the mouth.'

John D. Bargowski, Sr.

Chewing the Host

We marched in two
rows arranged boy-
girl-boy-girl up
the carpeted aisle
passed the glazed
stare of the stained
glass saints until
we reached the altar
rail and knelt on
the padded marble step.
Sister Phyllis emerged
from the sacristy,
her black cloak
streamed behind her
as she paced the altar
and commanded us *not*
to chew the host.
Let it melt slowly
in your mouth.
Close your eyes,
fold your hands
and point them
toward Heaven,
then swallow.
Warned us that
she would be watching
us Sunday afternoon,
carefully lifted
the crisp white wafers

between her thumb
and forefinger as one
by one we offered
our tongues to her
body of Christ, then
whirled and sprung
on Richie Papp caught
chewing the host
two days before
First Communion.
Richie Papp, who
every Sunday traded
the dime his mom
gave him to drop
in the poor-box
for a handful of Bazooka
bubble gum at Murray's,
stunned Sister, turned
her face bright
red so hot I thought
the glasses on her
face would shatter.
Sister shook Richie,
rattling the beads
on the rosary that
girded her waist,
and banished him
to the last pew,
and as I waited
for the melting host
planning my affected swallow
I could hear
the echoed crinkle
of his stubby fingers

peeling the wax
wrapper off another
chunk of gum.

David Oates

In the Garden

In the lot behind the parts store, the children play and examine abandoned headlines, broken root beer, outdated trust. They radiate over the lot, stopping to visit with the calico cat wearing a moustache stain from yesterday's berries. Back in the southwest corner, as far from the sale of antennas and general anesthesia as possible, they find a small garden. The store owner has rototilled and sprayed and hoed, and the wire cylinders are laden with homegrown tomatoes meditating on faith. There are also rows of other plantings: carrots, peas, Army colonels, skateboards with pink and yellow designs. The empty seed packets hang on popsickle sticks at the head of each row. The children walk along looking at packets, then stop and stare at one.

The faded paper has been scalded with images of babies. Of course the picture on the packet is of huge ripe babies, a bushel basketful, all 11 or 12 pounders with their flesh stretched tight by the sweet juice within. Sure enough, slow to sprout, a careful search reveals small heads forcing from the soil among large purple leaves. Even a few arms wave free, aimless. The children hear one crying, and run for fertilizer, hose, sprinkler attachment, tasteful curtains. They chant as the babies evolve, bloom, make elaborate patterns with their barely arms of cellophane-fine skin. The children gently peel away the leaves, examining the new faces. One plant is discharging its fruit feet first, little flat feet with pink pearls at one end.

The children run into the store, find the owner tinkering with a broken pasta maker which weeps quietly, steadily, olive oil tears flowing on its slick white label. They ask if they may pick some babies. "Please," said the owner. "In the winter I miss the fresh babies so. Then I plant too many. Next thing I know, I have babies all over the linoleum, bags and sacks and pots overflowing. Take as many as you like."

Back outside, the children quickly marry one another, burning sassafras roots, kneeling before the gooseneck lamps on the green altar, repeating the sacred jargon before drinking from the silver shovel. The brides wear yellow-and-black butterflies for bows, carry bouquets of coal and honey. Afterwards, they pull out a few last weeds and Valium from between the baby rows and go home to suppers in a range of suburban caves. They swallow savory meatloaf, baked chicken with tomatoes and tarragon, and ambitious shrimp. They pass through numerous station breaks. Yet none of it registers; they ride the dream of the shoots among purple leaves.

The next day they phone in sick and congregate in the garden. It's a clear day. The dew glitters as the luminous milkweed tacks past. Many babies are ripe, their bodies reddish, full, almost completely free of the plants. The children take a wheelbarrow around and pull the babies from thick blue stems inside the plants.

One plant is closed and swollen. It shakes every few moments. A bespectacled little boy with a new-potato nose produces his Scout knife. He slices a long neat line, goes back and forth in it smoothly, letting other children pull back the leaves already cut. From the severed edges of the plant oozes a sticky white sap which will take days to fully come off the children's hands. It smells of green plant with a slight stink of bitter mystery. He sticks his arms in like someone first up to the elbow in a Halloween pumpkin, forces his hands around the child there, roots it out, then holds it high with a great smile twisting the left side of his face.

The seed packet picture hadn't exaggerated much. The ripe babies they've found are eight pounds or more, lovely, well formed. The pickers handle the plants gently so that the flowers and small, hard greenish babies are not disturbed. The owner should have plenty more.

Picking by herself is an energetic blonde girl with ears like pink butterfly wings and a serious bud of a mouth. She pulls back the purple leaves of one plant and finds a misshapen baby. He lies still, with outsized head, divided lip, small, withered limbs and trunk. When he blinks and begins a weak cry she is almost sorry. Yet she picks him anyway. She lets the others finish the gathering. As she sits and holds this baby, she imagines throwing him in the back of the lot along with melted radios and empty Kool-Aid envelopes, choosing instead some ruddy little wrestler- or professor-to-be from the barrow. But she doesn't. She holds the baby, her long limp hair touching him and making a curtain around their two faces. She strokes him with her forefinger and coos, and something enters her heart like a robin swooping in, worm in beak.

The babies have dirt on them. Also weed and bug poisons. The children wash them in cola and rose water, anoint them with perfumes, pour the rarest oil on the new heads. The babies stare out with enormous concentration, licking the air like snakes tasting a scent. They are dressed in little suits and uniforms. The children throw a tea party, the babies sitting politely in their chairs. Imaginary tea with milk and sugar is served with cookies, duck eggs, and cake on the finest, most delicate plastic china.

The babies are growing at a great rate, and the children notice themselves aging. The teenagers and toddlers dance and sing. Sometimes it seems as if the younger ones merge into the older. Sometimes a child wanders from its child-become-parent, and they seem oblivious to each other; these children dance with other families. Mostly the children yo-yo from and to their parents.

The adults still wear the clothes they wore into the garden, though they now have ties and sensible shoes. Their clothes, and those of their children, expand with them. The blonde girl looks even older than the others, but the child she holds does not change, may even be dead. It is wrapped in white, and she feeds it from a bottle, though an I.V. bag drips nearby.

The other children wear football helmets and swimsuits, hold alphabet blocks and surveying instruments in their hands. The parents don't dance as long now. The old people sit as their children, grown tall and straight, work the garden, hauling babies in the owner's squeaking barrow. A little blonde child sits by her grandmother and holds her helpless uncle.

When the old people have withered down, their graying children have a tea party with them, dolloping sherry in the tea where it's wanted. They help their parents from their clothes. The loose wrinkled flesh is covered with dust and penicillin. Their children and grandchildren wash them with carrot juice and red wine, anoint them with perfumes, pour chrism on their heads. Then the families wrap the old people in great purple sheets sprinkled with gold dust, and lay them on the compost heap. As their ancient children sit and watch their own children and grandchildren work the garden, the snores from the purple-wrapped ancestors serenade them all.

Seymour Mayne

Milk

Joubert, the name popping off the bottles of milk in my youth.

The truck punctuates this wolf hour with false stops and starts.

If you are taking on new deliveries, please leave a bottle at the door. We need it. It is full of teeming memories and the nourishing taste of first partakings.

Lawrence Schimel

Journeybread Recipe

> *Even in the electric kitchen there was*
> *the smell of a journey.*
> — Anne Sexton, *"Little Red Riding Hood"*

1. In a tupperware wood, mix child and hood. Stir slowly. Add wolf.

2. Turn out onto a lightly floured path, and begin the walk home from school.

3. Sweeten the journey with candied petals: velvet tongues of violet, a posy of roses. Soon you will crave more.

4. Knead the flowers through the dough as wolf and child converse, tasting of each others flesh, a mingling of scents.

5. Now crack the wolf and separate the whites—the large eyes, the long teeth—from the yolks.

6. Fold in the yeasty souls, fermented while none where watching. You are too young to hang out in bars.

7. Cover, and, warm and moist, let the bloated belly rise nine months.

8. Shape into a pudgy child, a dough boy, lumpy but sweet. Bake half an hour.

9. Just before the time is up—the end in sight, the water broken—split the top with a hunting knife, bone-handled and sharp.

10. Serve swaddled in a wolfskin throw, cradled in a basket and left on a grandmother's doorstep.

11. Go to your room. You have homework to be done. You are too young to be in the kitchen, cooking.

Melody Lacina

Danish Pumpernickel

You bite into its dense vowels
in the bakery on Domingo,
your tongue nearly tasting it
just by saying the name.
You ate pumpernickel
the year you were seventeen
studying in Denmark, the year
you left your family to learn to think
in another tongue. You want to eat
what you remember.
Loaf with the shape and heft of a brick.
The bread is hard to cut, like breaking
earth in winter. In Danish
there's a phrase that means cutting pumpernickel.
Something about horses.
You tell me this while I carve
slices thick as your thumb.
We don't talk about when we were lovers.
We put the ordinary between us.
Something we share by cutting or breaking.
Something as simple as bread.

Lorna Crozier

Domestic Scene

I mop the floors, admire again the grain,
the beautiful simplicity of wood.
The cat we named Nowlan after the poet
who just died, cries for his tin of fish.
You stuff our salmon with wild rice
and watercress, its flesh pink
as Nowlan's mouth, his perfect tongue.
How lucky we are to have found each other,
our fine grey cat, a fresh Atlantic salmon.
Tomorrow we may get drunk and fight
or buy two tickets to Madrid.
But tonight the light in our kitchen
is as good as you'll find anywhere.
The plates glow with possibilities
and the cat licks himself completely clean.

Alden Nowlan

And He Wept Aloud, So That the Egyptians Heard It

In my grandfather's house
for the first time in years,
houseflies big as bumblebees
playing crazy football
in the skim-milk-coloured windows,

leap-frogging from
the cracked butter saucer
to our tin plates of
rainbow trout and potatoes, catching the bread
on its way to our mouths,
       mounting one another
       on the rough deal table.

It was not so much their filth
as their numbers and persistence and—
oh, admit this, man, there's no point in poetry
if you withhold the truth
once you've come by it—
       their symbolism:
       Baal-Zebub,
god of the poor and outcast,

that enraged me, made me snatch the old man's
Family Herald, attack them like a maniac,
lay to left and right until the window sills
overflowed with their smashed corpses,
until bits of their wings
stuck to my fingers,
until the room buzzed with their terror...

And my grandfather, bewildered, and afraid,
came to help me:
>   "never seen a year
>   when the flies were so thick"
as though he'd seen them at all before I came!

His voice so old and baffled and pitiful
that I threw my club into the wood box and sat down
>   and wanted to beg his forgiveness
as we ate on in silence broken only
by the almost inaudible humming
of the flies rebuilding their world.

Susan Ioannou

77th Birthday Dinner
for my father

The chandelier trembles.
Cling to the velvet-flocked walls
holding back death.
Flag down the maitre d' with a handkerchief napkin,
jab a tarnished fork in the oysterless shell.

Why must bones snap brittle as crusts,
breath sour to lukewarm wine?
Send back the overripe camembert.
Rattle your cup at the curdled cream.

Death creeps over the tablecloth nonetheless,
nibbles at your fingertips,
gnaws on the limp yellow rose.
Demand the bill be tallied again,
no tip on the Absolut, after taxes.
Refuse to let the captain pull back your chair.

The dining room closes at midnight.
Stop our clocked hearts if you can.

Barbara Crooker

Picking Sour Pie Cherries

I

Blue envelope.
The letter's come from Florida,
as I knew it would, soon
after your last one telling
how his heart kept stopping,
how the machines couldn't keep him
much longer. You were married
fifty-seven years.

II

Today it's the height of June,
and I'm picking sour cherries
to put by for pies.
Here in the north,
they need that snow
to run with juice.
Each red globe pulls away,
flesh from stone
only when ripe.
Such sweetness in our bodies,
what's sure, what's tangible.

III

At the sink, I push the pits
out with my thumb.
How did this fruit come

from such small flowers,
delicate lace,
spring snow drifting
from bough to bough?

IV

I am making pie crust,
cutting lard into flour and salt;
the floor is white with flurries.
Whatever cracks can be pinched and patched.
I stir the cherries with sugar and butter,
a bowlful of garnets shines in the pan.
Fancy with lattice-work, crimped-in designs,
I make this in his memory,
your life and mine, the tart, the bitter, the sweet.

Heather Spears

Bulimia Poem

Pebbles on North Beach—it's the old brain
said Hallie as she stooped to collect
ringed ones, I went for the white.
Thousands of thousands newly banked
in the diurnal washes, combed and patternless,
bright with the scour, the burnishing. That brain
delights in singling out, she said. The eye
darts and instantly it's there, the nip,
the primate appositional.
Robert at Ocean Park
would walk for agates, breakwater to point,
never breaking his stride,
lift them unerring out of the sparkled trash
of barnacles, granite, sugar-stones.
Our gatherer's heritage, she said.
Not learned, still there on hold,
ancient necessity.

And now salmonberries,
all morning in head high
tunneling trails at Sooke—
flies buzz, the sea sushes, all that dapple and sun
yellow and crimson loosening fruit
heeded and eaten without thought,
abundant, watery, near tasteless. Tonight
this intricate play of leaf and light's
harvest will press at my eyes—oh good, good brain,
to keep such pictures in its picture book!

Why not a fat farm just to praise
bulimia? women would come
surprised by normalcy, and out among
the berries wander with uncut hair
lifting their bare arms in the oldest dance
picking till dusk into their happy mouths,
what's left they'll spread red-handed, pound
to Salish bannock for grayish men to show
in the Anthropo
logical
Museum in Victoria, and laugh, and hold
their basins firm between their thighs.
And all night long lie in white rows
in a chaste dormitory, forgiven,
and watch their brains' blessed page
illuminated like a bestiary.

Anne F. Walker

Sloe berries

> . . . *after the "iceman," unearthed in the Alps in 1992, in whose pockets sloe berries and medicinal mushrooms were found.*

Imprinted leaves of blossoms
on small blue plums. Body pulled
from the glacier.

The mirror frightening in
any unexpected door.
Oval form
idikon frost.

Margaret Atwood

Late August

This is the plum season, the nights
blue and distended, the moon
hazed, this is the season of peaches

with their lush lobed bulbs
that glow in the dusk, apples
that drop and rot
sweetly, their brown skins veined as glands

No more the shrill voices
that cried *Need Need*
from the cold pond, bladed
and urgent as new grass

Now it is the crickets
that say *Ripe Ripe*
slurred in the darkness, while the plums

dripping on the lawn outside
our window, burst
with a sound like thick syrup
muffled and slow

The air is still
warm, flesh moves over
flesh, there is no

hurry

Brenda Hillman

Trois Morceaux en Forme de Poire
Titled after Satie

I.
Three pears ripen
On the ledge. Weeks pass.
They are a marriage.

The middle one's the conversation
The other two are having.
He is their condition.

Three wings without birds,
Three feelings.
How can they help themselves?

They can't.
How can they stay like that?
They can.

II.
The pears are consulting.
Business is bad this year,

D'Anjou, Bartlett.
They are psychiatrists,

Patient and slick.
Hunger reaches the hard stem.

It will get rid of them.

III.
The pears are old women;
They are the same.
Slight rouge,
Green braille dresses,
They blush in unison.
They will stay young.
They will not ripen.
In the new world,
Ripeness is nothing.

Kelly Cherry

Woman Living Alone

A book on the bed,
radio turned to a classical station.

Raining or not raining, but if it is, the water rushes
into the bushes by the side of the brick house,

bridal wreath bushes, their white flowers
like snow in spring.

If it is not raining,
there may be a blue sky like a blessing

being pronounced over a meal, which,
though taken alone,

tastes of life.

Patricia Monaghan

Snow White on the Apple

I held it up, solid in my hands,
flesh of the tree, dense as rock,
gleaming like crimson secrets.

It smelled like earth spice.
It smelled like dusky water.
It smelled like the ghost of roses.

Of course I knew it was the apple
of forgetfulness. But oh, sister,
how much I needed to forget:

the assaults, the betrayals,
the abandonments. I did not bite
into that fruit in ignorance.

This is exactly what I wanted:
stillness, glassy beauty, peace.
This is exactly what I wanted.

Marie Henry

Onions

It was the year she came to love onions. She couldn't get enough of them... dug them up out of the field, slept with them under her pillow, hid in the pantry at night so she could count them. She piled them up in bins and baskets, moving them from one corner to the other. Soon, there was not enough room in the pantry. She moved them out into the living room, organized them by color and shape. The dried outer skins drifted about the floor like spring snow.

She sang to them, checked on them often to make sure they were all right. At night, she held them up to the moon.

The onion lady moved in and out of the seasons, squeezed the onions of their milk so she could rub it into her skin. She placed an onion in the hollow underneath each arm, carried them around like small birds tucked away in their nests.

Next year, she would move into the garden.

Christine Erwin

Diamond Cloves

I'm going to mend your heart with broccoli, sew on delicate beads of cheese, and with lemon cake meet you down in my arms. You'll be amazed. You'll be drunk on cinnamon and diamond cloves. Tiny chickens in broth will weave cobwebs of butter and orange round your head, while I offer glistening curries, and soups that you'll sip with a silver spoon, that you'll sigh to finish. Have another dollop of sour cream. At first you'll be polite, watch from an armchair as I click-clack to the oven, to the top shelf of the cupboard, but after a taste of willing asparagus, or a bite of tomato, you'll move closer, hover. Sauces thickening your breath, a tang of salt on your bursting lips, and I'll have you. You won't know how, you'll think it's love.

opal palmer adisa

Nature's Feast

the sun is
gluttonous
every jamaican day
him *nyam* my body
mawing away
like a possessed painter
stabbing his canvas
with bold colors
is mackerel-run-down
him think me is
salty and sugary

the sea is
insatiable
forever thirsty
every time i visit
she gulp me down
washing me in she belly
she say water
is life
and me is
sweet coconut-water
sprinkled with a dash
of rum

the wind is
more particular
him like to savor
him food
folding me in the curl

of him tongue
him suck and smack
and hold me in
him mouth like
a toothless man
chewing on coconut-drops

father time is
relentless
patient as the moon
him is a connoisseur
sampling   grouping
selecting utensils
adding condiments
but sometimes
father time
is a *maku* man
that does hide
and devour
him catch raw
oysters swimming
in vinegar and pepper

Andrea Adolph

Salt Eater

> *for Annette*

Like a hangover
you say, as if daylight
would find the cupboards
empty, a fifth
on its side,
your chin sticky with Jamaican rum.

It's what you crave.
You lick the tops
off a boxful
of Cheese Nips, add
soy sauce when no one
is watching.

Mornings, crystals
have gathered to a thud
in your temples, fingers
grown over their rings,
eyes amphibian
in a slow blink.

Elise M. McClellan

Lamia Bulimia

I do it like sex with two fingers.
I know how to toggle the switch,
twitching muscles tightly
My neck spread far between head and breasts.
I know opening.
I've practiced with legs and eyes,
anus and joints,
motion over limbs.
My hand falls over chin, clutching jaw
stroking the choke
throttling throat raw.

I do it because addiction tastes like salt,
the cool blades of my fingers
sheathing for purity.
I do it because I am Raphaelite rapturous,
foam-bodied, Botticelli's Venus--
I do it because food is my enemy.
No matter how small I chew the bits,
they gather at my belly and hips.
I do it because eating is sex
and I love sex.

But men don't bed godess bodies in the 90's.
I puke, I cry, I shake.
I pull my hair back and lean and lean.
Sometimes strands fall through the gag

and I carry the scent of possible thinness.
It's like coming through teeth.
And being numbed, emptied,
Flushed.

Lorna Crozier

Eggs

Mary won't eat chicken
because she dreamed a hen
with her daughter's head
spoke to her.

She takes this for an omen
and why not? What's more female
than a hen, its rosary of eggs
growing inside, each
a memory of self,
a first genesis, the yolk
spotted with blood—
an image held in our brains
before our birth.

There's something about chickens.
As a child I loved to clean them,
push my hand into the cavity
(like the space I knew
inside me) pull out the guts,
the heart, the gizzard with its stones,
the tiny eggs warm in my palm.

Nothing was like the diagrams
in our health texts in school.
In the kitchen there was shit
if the skin of the intestines broke
and always there was blood.

The blood that made me
bend in pain
was a secret no one talked about.
Then I was the daughter.
                    My head
separate from my body
knew more of a chicken's
than my own.

Maureen Eppstein

Squid

It's easy to fix a squid
the cook book said
economical too
first pull off the head
and the tentacles
peel the pink-spotted skin
I am taking your personhood squid
now make sure it's clean inside
I am the clinical finger
pushing us inside out
you are your own rubber glove
your jelly and clots
a morning diaphragm

what a neat vagina they cooed
here's a nice little cap
I cried in the john
when it wouldn't go in
and the rats
scratched at the wall

your squid will be now all milky white
and not at all scary
the cook book said
no not at all scary
a heap of discarded condoms
flopped in a dish
and opaque unquestioning eyes
gazing up from the sink

Susan Ioannou

Potato Lethargy

Each month
behind my eyelids
sprouts a giant potato

puffing up
hands and middle
from roots in waterfull feet.

Without ever moving
I widen
I rise.

How many like me
taste this
vegetable essence

and long for that first stab
paring skin back
to size?

M. Carmen Santos

marinade

As the radio warbles an advertisement for monster trucks she
pulls back the skin back on the breasts, rubs lime into the opals
of meat, caresses the whole carcass. The bite of citrus
delivers island brochure getaways and sunburn; the juice
piercing a hangnail as she fingers the ridges on the inside
of a bird, revealing the entrails for gravy.
This is a single woman's meal with rock cornish game hen.
Contact with poultry can be more specific
than a man's hungry voice.

Lorna Crozier

Childhood

Close your eyes for a moment,
listen:
the floorboards groan at your mother's step,
bread pans scrape the oven grate,
her fingers tap the crust.
Where are you now?
Pretending sleep in another room
where windows turn dreams to frost,
feather forests, the birds are white
and make no sound.

Listen: your mother pours milk in a cup.
It holds the light like a small lamp,
draws shadows from her face.
Where have you gone?
Your mother is calling.
Your name is warmed by her breath.
Snow fills your tracks,
turns everything into a softer shape,
a silence, forgiveness.

Come in for supper,
it is growing dark.
A cup waits for you, a loaf of bread.
Your mother is calling, listen:
with her voice she builds a doorway
for you to enter, even now,
from such a long way off.

Elizabeth Follin-Jones

Leaks

Everywhere in the house
is the need for order.
The grandmother darns sheets
before the children finish
dreaming. The father returns
fish bones packed in his lunch.
The mother promises cake
even as she climbs a ladder
to strip off shingles
in her search for leaks.

Each day new gaps.
Windows give way to vines,
dolls languish, words drop
from sentences. The father
calls for sandbags, the children
plug holes with T shirts.
Soon the family is barely visible.

The mother uses her last match
to build a fire with old diaries.
Their warmth seduces her.
She fills the soup kettle
but before she can spoon broth
into the others' mouths, they have
disappeared with their lives.

Ronald Wallace

The Fat of the Land

Gathered in the heavy heat of Indiana,
summer and 102, we've come from
all over this great country,
one big happy family, back from
wherever we've spread ourselves too thin.
A cornucopia of cousins and uncles, grand-
parents and aunts, nieces and nephews, expanding.
All day we laze on the oily beach;
we eat all the smoke-filled evening:
shrimp dip and crackers,
Velveeta cheese and beer,
handfuls of junk food, vanishing.
We sit at card tables, examining
our pudgy hands, piling in
hot fudge and double chocolate
brownies, strawberry shortcake and cream,
as the lard-ball children
sluice from room to room.
O the loveliness of so much loved flesh,
the litany of split seams and puffed sleeves,
sack dresses and Sansabelt slacks,
dimpled knees and knuckles, the jiggle
of triple chins. O the gladness
that only a family understands,
our fat smiles dancing
as we play our cards right.
Our jovial conversation blooms and booms
in love's large company, as our sweet
words ripen and split their skins:
mulberry, fabulous, flotation

phlegmatic, plumbaginous.
Let our large hearts attack us,
our blood run us off the scale.
We're huge and whole on this simmering night,
battened against the small skinny
futures that must befall all of us,
the gray thin days and the non-caloric dark.

Wesley McNair

The Fat Enter Heaven

It is understood, with the clarity possible only
in heaven, that none have loved food
better than these. Angels gather to admire
their small mouths and their arms, round
as the fenders of Hudson Hornets. In their past
they have been among the world's most meek,
the farm boy who lived with his mother,
the grade-school teacher who led the flag salute
with expression, day after day. Now
their commonplace lives, the guilt about weight,
the ridicule fade and disappear.
They come to the table arrayed with perfect food,
shredding their belts and girdles for the last time.
Here, where fat itself is heavenly,
they fill their plates and float upon the sky.

Kelly Cherry

Lunch at the Lake

Bees are falling out of the sky,
Thick and heavy as honey.
The lake is as sour as rye.

Curdling in late summer, the lake
Is as sluggish as cream. Fish bake.
The sun is the color of a cornflake.

Fish float in on waves, already broiled.
They lie on their sides, dead to the world.
You own skin's well oiled.

You could die and be eaten, here
On the lakeshore wall, where
Bees are streaming through your hair

And fish are serving themselves up
On your lap, poisoned, and the paper cup
You drink from is alive, says the environmental commission, with
        denizens of the deep.

You could float through the lake like ice cream in Coke,
Brown cow, melt in the sun, and sink,
Current among currents, finally over the brink.

Beryl Baigent

Chernobyl Summer

That Summer
while I was buying sheers
for your living room
the Kremlin drew down
an iron curtain of secrecy
and the prevailing winds
blowing towards Sweden
veiled that country in
nuclear mist.

That Summer
while I was reading
"Predators of the Adoration"
and "How Hug a Stone"
the predators swarmed towards
Denmark, Poland, Czechoslovakia
and stones could do nothing
to prevent radiation from reaching
the underground water table.

That Summer
while the warm sun
shimmered over the
Canadian landscape
Europe smouldered under
a residue of fear.
While we banqueted on
garden peas, tomatoes
corn and strawberries

over there   milk from
grass-eating cows was banned
and thousands consumed iodine tablets
to hinder the body's absorption.
Others needing deeper nourishment
prayed for bone marrow
transplants to treat their
special kind of sickness.

Not panic but vigilance
caused them to build
a concrete tomb around
the corpse of radioactive dust.
And here   we are instructed
not to drink our rainwater
the Bequerel index
having recorded more than
ten b per litre.

That Summer
we clung to each other in gratitude
aware of our healthy bones and hair
grateful for the heavy rain
which washed away the fallout.
That Summer
like the butterfly
we counted not months but moments
and had time enough.

Susan Bumps

Giving Homage to the Summer Fruit God

Teapots for sale
and all of us aching for apricots
our faces smudged with summer dust.
Here, in this town, it means nothing.
We are only like so many other
overheated tourists
longing for fast food restaurants
and their cool artificial comfort.
Out here, on this road stretching
like a half starved giraffe
I alone am content to feel the grit
layering my skin, my hair
the heat wafting up in waves
as if we were all a little too close
to central-heating's open winter vents.

Inside the small store,
cluttered with bent, finger-smudged
postcards,
I write my name in teapot dust
trace my finger along the letter outlines
over and over and over
as if by some magic, my intense rubbing
could invoke a rain spirit
to wipe away
the age of this town.

Oh, how good apricot juice would sound,
would look as it gushed ripe—dripped down our faces

forming rivulets in the dust
like journeys yet taken.

With our last damp crumpled dollars
we buy bags full,
though they aren't as cold as we'd like
and shove them into our dry mouths
savoring the soft flesh
and not even bothering
to watch out for bruises.

Rachel Blau DuPlessis

T

The tea cup in the soft lamp light
travels its little tea breath and milky waves,
its train of time, sentimentally.

I'm thirsty. And it was a question.
    And something   To which the answer is:
                                    there is no "beauty."

           ties
           tries   it.
           tires

                         I can't get myself
Faced   *the simplest things*
                     make yourself a cup of tea
with the tarballs   *somehow*
                   I have to get thru this I cringe
                   every day I cringe
                   It's like living in a tomb.

officials are taking a wait and see
attitude.

Donia Blumenfeld Clenman

Shortbread Cookies

to my mother

Your body dust.
The bones decaying.
I do not think of you often.

Sipping tea,
caramel fudge before me,
I suddenly long
for your shortbread cookies.

Ioanna-Veronika Warwick

Chocolate Hearts
for Franek

In my teens I was crazy
about chocolate hearts—
gingerbread
dipped in dark delight.
They could be bought
only in Pomerania;
were baked in Torun,
that gingerbread town.
My Pomeranian

cousin sent them to me,
a special food parcel to Warsaw.
I'd eat three at once,
luscious and rich brown,
then ration the supply:
one heart a day,
in small bites.
Sometimes I'd moisten
one corner in tea.
So what if Father laughed
that I ate like a grandma.

Ah, and the soft
heart of the heart!
It's been a quarter of a century.
A doctor told me I shouldn't
eat chocolate or drink tea.
As if it could ever
be the same.

Doctor, I am in danger.
I cannot tell
truth from memory.
I know everything has changed.
Perhaps they no longer
make those hearts.

Perhaps only I
remember them, an inexact
phantasmagoria of pleasure,
the citizens as usual
(not everything has changed),
obsessed with politics.

I left in part to get away
from politics.
Life always seemed to me
larger than that,
meaning closer to the self.
The small things that become
the scripture of the absolute.

Memory can lie.
We demand deeper meaning,
not this gingerbread façade.
I could say,
"The chocolate was bitter as tears,
the hunger could not be filled—"
or, "Torun where Copernicus was born,
'the man who stopped the sun'—"

They were gingerbread
with lime-blossom honey,
wrapped in cellophane
and stamped with the price.

Reader, I know you suspect
this is a bitter-sweet
tale about my own heart.
The way I kiss,
slowly, in small bites.
The way I tell stories,
saving for later the soft parts.
Everything is symbolic,
but once it was real.
I said luscious, brown.

Linda Pastan

Pears

Some say
it was a pear
Eve ate.
Why else the shape
of the womb,
or of the cello
whose single song is grief
for the parent tree?
Why else the fruit itself
tawny and sweet
which your lover
over breakfast
lets go your pear-
shaped breast
to reach for?

Diana O'Hehir

Apple

I examine the cut-open center with its darkly outlined
Double aura. Poking out of that is a seed, a small
Love point, a repetition
Of the pattern of sex.

This apple is symmetrical, with a neat curved stem.
The waxed outside the bright infertile green
Of artificial grass, the flesh
Bland, blank; molecules pressed so close
Their edges have merged.

But still, again and again, on all things growing, that pattern.

She stands naked in her garden, her red hair
Down over her shoulders, her freckled hand
Extended. Adam, she says . . .
Bird shift in the tree, turn
Their blue and scarlet tails under, leaves incline,
Each one spills a drop of moisture,
The small wind pauses, makes a bubble of stillness around
Her body, his body,
The apple green globe sits on her palm
All the light of steamy Paradise collects around it.

Adam bends his head. It's the world's perfume he's
Breathing in. It's the skin of that world
He sinks his teeth into.

Kelly Cherry

Lt. Col. Valentina Vladimirovna Tereshkova
first woman to orbit the earth,
June 16-June 19, 1963

It looked like an apple
or a Christmas orange:
I wanted to eat it.
I could taste the juice
trickling down my throat,
my tongue smarted,
my teeth were chilled.
How sweet those mountains seemed,
how cool and tangy, the Daugava!

What scrawl of history
had sent me so far from home? . . .

When I was a girl in school, comrades,
seemingly lazy as a lizard
sprawled on a rock in Tashkent,
I dreamed of conquest.
My hands tugged at my arms,
I caught flies on my tongue.

Now my soul's as hushed as the Steppes on a winter night;
snow drifts in my brain, something
shifts, sinks, subsides inside,

and some undying pulse hoists my body
like a flag, and sends me up,
like Nureyev.
From my samovar I fill my cup with air,

and it overflows.
Who knows who scatters the bright cloud?

Two days and almost twenty-three hours
I looked at light,
scanning its lines like a book.

My conclusions:

At last I saw the way
time turns,
like a key in a lock,
and night becomes a day,
and sun burns away the primeval mist,
and day is, and is not.

Listen, earthmen,
comrades of the soil,
I saw the Black Sea shrink to a drop
of dew and disappear;
I could blot out Mother Russia with my thumb in thin air;
the whole world was nearly not there.

It looked like an apple
or a Christmas orange:
I wanted to eat it.
I thought, It is pleasant to the eyes,
good for food,
and eating it would make men and women wise.

I could taste the juice
trickling down my throat,
my tongue smarted,
my teeth were chilled.

How sweet those mountains seemed,
how cool and tangy, the Daugava!

Mary di Michele

from "Crown of Roses"

26

The moon is half
              full (or half
gone) the moon is round,
                    stoneground, a peasant loaf
sweetened with golden corn,
              mealy and moist,
a peasant loaf when divided, when devoured
                              at the feast for which
you arrive too late.

Hunger makes even crumbs glow
                    as brilliantly as wishing
stars. In the dark the moon
dazzles more than the sun
                    (for which we feel less need)
all night long Sappho
              i also sleep alone . . .

Alphonse Daudet

Polenta

translated by J. Weintraub

The Corsican coast, a November evening.—We land during the heavy rains, in a wild, solitary land. Some charcoal burners from Lucca make room for us at their fire; then a local shepherd, sort of a wild man dressed all in goat skin, invites us into his shed to eat polenta. We enter stooping, shrinking, inside a hut where you can't even stand up straight. In the middle, some sticks of green wood are flaring between four black stones. The smoke escaping from them climbs toward the hole bored into the hut, then swells out everywhere, beaten back by the wind and the rain. A small lamp— the Provençal *caleil*—opens a timid eye into this stifling air. A woman, children appear from time to time when the smoke clears, and from the depths, a pig grunts. The debris from shipwrecks can be discerned, a bench made from the fragments of hulls, a wooden crate with faded lettering, a mermaid's head of painted wood torn from some prow, washed clean by seawater.

The polenta is atrocious. The chestnuts, poorly ground, have a moldy taste. They must have lain for too long beneath the trees, open to the rain. Afterwards comes the white Corsican cheese, with its wild taste that makes you reflect upon vagabond goats. We are here in a misery fully Italian. Hardly a house, this refuge. The weather so fine, the life so easy. Nothing but a kennel for the heavy rains. And then who cares about the smoke, and flickering lamp, since it is understood that a roof means prison and that you can't live well except in the full light of the sun?

Edward Wolf

Comfort Food

Somewhere I'd heard that expression before—'comfort food'—but
I'd never really thought about it. And I'm no cook — but it turns out
I can dish up comfort food. Know what that is? French toast, rice
pudding, cupcakes; something soft, warm, sweet. Of course I'm
trying to be clever with this too, clever enough to get him to eat, eat
anything. I could never have imagined what a 106 pound man
would look like. Studying the anatomy of my 44 year old friend,
everything on the surface. The skin so stretched out—for the first
time I really see where leather comes from. And bones. The wrist is
so big, the cheek is so delicate. Large pots of soup and an angel food
cake. Anything. Anything he wants. I dragged an old upholstered
chair into the garden and covered it with tarps at night. When he
can, he sits in it in the morning light and drinks hot chocolate (I
made it from scratch) and drifts in and out. The garden is full of
nasturtiums this year and I suddenly remember a salad we had once
in a restaurant in North Beach. Someone had put a handful of
orange nasturtiums in it. A salad of flowers. Now I'm wondering
what else I could make that will work.

Sandra McPherson

Food

I

Tell me again how the bureaucrats drive to the forest
and eat oxalis, how they go ambling alone,
bending down to the plumose green floor, choosing one leaf
to start with and chewing it up, bitter but changing to tart,
how they finish that one and break off another viridian
warfere and persist, weaving like insects, having no office

II

but to eat. Berries are what the escapees ate. Detectives
found one, a robber named Gardener, purple-stained
beneath a car. Berry canes end in knuckles to kiss. If a con
breaks jail in August, berries are waiting to help,
the ones you told me not to swallow, by the Reynolds
aluminum plant. A fine unrustable dust
toxic on its black sugar, the first tasted superb, each one

III

satisfied my thirst. Free food: is it so ungoverned,
so unbusinesslike? Three hundred shaggy manes
I picked in a park, truckloads of groceries the Symbionese
forced Hearst to give away, those two unpaid-for Cokes
that rolled to my dime from their machine.
The poor line up on the fish pier. Jane and I pluck bay leaves
from the hills that bottle reservoirs. I want to sample

IV

Indian salad: red ants crawling over miner's lettuce—
bodies shaken off, their formic acid dresses the greens
like vinegar. It's not a freezer full of venison. Or our
Thanksgiving table costing ammunition: glazed pheasant, nutmeated
squirrel, rabbits tarragoned in a pot. Not chutney-roasted quail.
But sorrel—woodsy salad of waterfalls. It bites back.

V

It's not what Richard Hugo told me once: "Those hitchhikers
I let ride with me because it was Wyoming
later were detained with fingers in their pockets,
fingers not their own. What a meal I would have made!"
No, I go and take no one, up-mountain with the oxalis.
It grows in the shade but folds up on dark days,
like a person losing love losing appetite. I have tried it
both ways.

Ronald Wallace

The Dinner Party

Everyone out in the living room's concerned
about groundwater and nuclear war,
their voices a warm glow in the dark,
the familiar country of engaging party talk,
and I'm here in the kitchen with my spinach
and my eggs, my vinegar and oil, worrying

about how to make a salad. Worrying
is something I'm very good at. I've been concerned
over things much less important than spinach
which at this moment seems worse than war.
How much easier, I think, it is to talk
than actually do something. I'm in the dark

about this salad. Shall I add these dark
olives, these tomatoes? Should I be worrying
the oil into the vinegar? Do I talk
to the eggs and parsley, show my concern
to the celery? The ingredients are at war
as I wonder whether this is lettuce or spinach.

As a child I hated salads, hated spinach.
One night I was sent to my lonely dark
room for dawdling, not eating. A family war
erupted, my father shouting, my mother worrying
that I'd be damaged for life, her concern
radiating up through the floor. Their talk

filled the house with tear gas, talk
that tasted in my mouth worse than spinach.

I wished they had something else to be concerned
about, as I fled through the foreign dark
of their anger. They could have been worrying
about Hitler and the Second World War.

Out in the living room they've moved from war
to gourmet cooking in that easy way talk
has of absolving itself of all worry
in time. And now it's time for spinach.
Let groundwater keep its own dark
counsel, radiation be its own concern.

This is war. I serve up the goddamned spinach.
All talk ceases in the leafy dark.
On their lips: the oil of concern, the vinegar of worry.

Kathleen Evans

The Starving Woman in Four Parts

<u>Part 1</u>
At twenty four I ate
one potato a day for three weeks,
a microwaved wrinkled turd
shriveling, empty, flat like me
and my husband so proud of my rejecting
and deflating

At twenty I ate nothing in October.
After class I'd drift to dizzy sleep
my hipbones little unshucked shrimps poking the mattress springs
my eyes growing fast as cancer,
big in a tight, wan face
I hadn't taken a shit in weeks
my dormmates commended my success

At fifteen Nancy and I did the banana diet (3 one-banana meals
daily)
the sunflower seed diet (unlimited woody, gum-jabbing seeds)
the chicken diet (3 one-wing meals daily)
the laxative diet, crapping out every last morsel
Our collarbones lifted the spaghetti straps of our prom dresses
Our breats rolled like small firm olives between our boyfriends'
fingers

<u>Part 2</u>
During the starving I get dizzy, organized
Listlessly I make lists:
       five favorite foods to consume when the starving is over
       ten nails to polish

fifteen miles to run
twenty hair curlers to buy
thirty jokes to laugh at
forty days and nights to rain on a man

Part 3
Suddenly I cannot get enough food, or talking, or debts, or daiquiris,
or freedom, or earrings, or talk shows, or long mornings on the toilet
reading *Cosmo*.   The pacing sets in, pacing of the bedroom,
dormroom, apartment cell, a container of whatever, hot or cold in
my hands, the strongest zoo lion contained in the smallest cage,
pacing to her racing heart, eyes concealing nothing.

Part 4
The cell filling begins, crowding in, invading
my still starving, bursting womanhood:
my hips become ripe plums mashing into the mattress
my breasts brim over my bra
my collarbones sink like an island
my stomach pulls its horsehead forward
my benign eyes melt waxlike into a fleshy face.

To face facing the face is the last part
known now by heart.

Barabara A. Hendryson

Before Poetry

Here's the newspaper photo, *Exotic Recipe Contest,*
annoncement I've won first prize. My marital hair
is curled 60's style, orderly as the sweater

. I wear--pale color, high necked, prim. I present,
for the camera, my platter of paella: succulent saffron
rice, lacing of garlic, olive oil, passion of herb

and spice, weaving of shrimp and clam. Then
the golden nugget of chicken, the ruddy pepper,
the briny fat green olive: the food of sex.

That was before poetry. My life, being free
and singular now, I gather another language,
like sea shells partly buried in coastal dunes.

Some, clearly mine; others toss and polish
in my hands until they are liquid, familiar, earned,
sweet on my tongue. I mound sand and shell

for a castle, a poem, like paella's golden rice.
Shell becomes olive, chicken, clam: word and
sound tossed on the tongue, edible as poetry.

Sarah Gail Johnson

Lunch
for Rachel

I try not to look at your fingers anymore.
Weighted under heavy shells
of polish, sick pink against brittle knuckles,
holding the single apple you swallow down
each day like a tight gold coin clinking
sharply in your hollow tin stomach; your smile
not filling up with softball
and hips and boyfriends but
a weak orange juice smile,
the beating heart of a girl watered down to
teeth and lipstick carefully chewing
the same bite slowly, slowly
chewing herself down to
the core.
Far hidden in the thirsty soil like diamonds
there are gleaming seeds bleeding
to death, they scream
take this food, you have
one last breath.

Leonore Wilson

Eating

I eat as if the embryo is still in me,
as if my child with its heart in its mouth
needs my nourishment. I eat
imagining the body stalk
joining the yolk sac. I see the future
spine thickening, the tail
bending and breaking off.
I imagine the groove curl
becoming tunnel, becoming
brain stem and spinal
cord. I eat
thinking I am needed, remembering that
period in my life when I was most
desired, when I was all animal,
mammal, expanding universe. I was
God. In those early days,
food was my only duty. I was sister
to the milk cow and slopped hog.
My figure was never girl. I was
all affection and compliment. I married
my call. In servitude
I knew freedom. I was not
woman nor female. I held the
world. I pulled a new language
from inside my uterus.
Corpus luteum, ripening follicle,
tough plug of mucus.
There were shifts in me
and migrations. I eat
thinking of my shimmering

placenta, my maternal
blood, those dark passages
becoming bone. I eat
thinking of the child
moving in me, his thumb
preparing that space
where my nipple will go.
I eat dreaming of that wild
greasy skin, that blue liquid,
that gathering heartbeat.
I eat as if I were waiting
for my first sweet air.

Hayley R. Mitchell

Mother's Milk

My sister's breasts
swell and ache
under the heavy gaze
of hungry inlaws
while her unborn child
sleeps unaware
of their expectations
their need
for that white
milky passing
of nutrients
from red, full nipples
to infant lips

Never mind
that she is scared
uninterested
or like *our* mother
repulsed
by thoughts of her child
sucking
like an animal
a pink piglet
in a public restroom
She is pressured to pump
lectured
as though her flow
will create the stars
fill the life giving waters
nourish *all* dry-mouthed babes

Deliver, sister
then take your secret pills
to dry and harden
the breats that swing
as a burden now
Your child will never know
the difference
and your inlaws that hope
to grow fat from your milk
can afford to go
hungry awhile

Kathleen Evans

Revolution

You heard your ex-husband
and his wife
will host a Christmas
dinner.
You're sure
the men will
spill crumbs on
brown couches
as they
eat hors-d'œuvres
and watch football
while the women slice
turkey
in the kitchen,
debating
if they
will rejoin
Jenny Craig
or Weight Watchers
or just run themselves
into the ground at the stroke
of January.

Once, in the kitchen,
your mother-
in-
law
asked you
to put
toothpaste

on his
toothbrush
each night,
placing it on the
bathroom sink
so
he
will
brush
more.

She gave you
a mix
master
that Christmas.

He gave you
jeans and
a gauze blouse
two sizes
too small.

After
dinner the men
crowd in the kitchen,
clank
the dishes
as they wash,
then pick their
teeth
with toothpicks
that she placed
in little
red
and

green
toothpick
holders.

It's not
the revolution
you thought it was going to be.

Rosemary Sullivan

The Table

Nobody planned this
table stretching its broad grin
across the floor, loaded with lives.

It's the house. Some nights
it wants. We come,
pulled by a stronger will,
unwittingly, to family
its geography of need.

Santiago's in the kitchen
hacking thin potato slivers
crisp, ambiguous as memories,
placed like wafers on our plates.
They are an augury. We squirm,
a thin laughter rises in the heat.

Adriana watches the lampshade
swing a hex across the ceiling.
One night she tied her husband to his bed,
eyes propped open with toothpicks,
while she took another man.
It was revenge he had to see.

Her son Sergito guards the door.
His father's disappeared.
In his tiny mind the memory climbs.
He beats a drum in anger,
takes pennies from a jar,
holds them over open palms,

a practised ritual, pulling back
before the pennies drop. He knows
already to withhold.

Ricardo plays the guru of the kitchen.
If you paint a balloon with dots
collapse it to one point,
that's the space and time. The centre
nowhere. Everywhere the centre.
The universe contracted to a table.

We play at the illusion
of a moment. The house
erupts:
oasis in our scattering.

Anne Barney

Kitchen Dichotomy

Making dinner after a baby's death
seems so unnecessary
to the mother.

She would eat popcorn
or rolled up slices of cheese,
and call it dinner.

The father, on the other hand,
sees it as something essential.
He wants to believe

he can still walk in the front door
and share a well-balanced home-
cooked meal at the same old kitchen table

with the same old wife who smiles
just to see him
enjoying his food.

John B. Lee

The Two Thousand Piece Popcorn Puzzle

I know a husband and wife
who spent an entire year of evenings
fitting together
the two thousand pieces of a popcorn puzzle
working at the kitchen table
like tax adjusters, tinkering
archaeologists with the ossified bones
of a busted Jurassic bird,
but when it was finished
they simply took a photograph of their labour
and tossed the jigsaws fracturing
back into the box
the pieces popping into fragments
of the whole
like a Saturday night without butter.

Felicia Mitchell

Eggs

> *Marriage isn't what it's cracked up to be.*
> —from a letter from my ex-husband

The last time we tried to scramble
brown yard eggs fresh in from the morning,
dew glistening like tears in a disappointed wife's eyes,
you cracked one up, the shell crumbling into yolk.
Hands trembling, overzealous, you tried again
in a second bowl, tapping the egg on porcelain;
half ended up spilling, spotting the tablecloth.
The only solution was to let the cat in to clean up,
get in the car, and go out to breakfast with deer hunters.

Another time, when I refused to leave the house for a week,
my grief a miscarriage, your sperm condemned,
as clumsy as your hands it seemed if my egg could not develop,
you called your mother and told her I was cracking up.
Like a yard egg, maybe, seeping through gingham onto oak,
cat lapping at my guts before I could harden.

And when I left you, I laughed for a week, free,
slap happy and half crazy at the idea of freedom,
a woman again on the run, no failed mother, my sanity
like a brown yard egg forgotten to the brood hen
setting a little too far back from the kitchen door.

Hayley R. Mitchell

Suzie gets a colander

all wrapped in bells
and silver bows
to match the stainless
steel handles,
Guaranteed
to not fall off,
the gloating gift giver says,
blue-haired
and ringless,
alone on the couch,
It's the best.
Mine's lasted forever.

Suzie squeals
like her first pink
Christmas ham,
squirms in her seat
like a strained carrot,
holds the colander
to her chest
for the sheer joy
of each night's vegetables,
while I sit back,
my faith in marriage
slipping easily
through all those holes.

Lorna Crozier

Carrots

Carrots are fucking
the earth. A permanent
erection, they push deeper
into the damp and dark.
All summer long
they try so hard to please.
Was it good for you,
was it good?

Perhaps because the earth won't answer
they keep on trying.
While you stroll through the garden
thinking *carrot cake*
carrots and onions in beef stew,
carrot pudding with caramel sauce,
they are fucking their brains out
in the hottest part of the afternoon.

Carol V. Davis

Garden

I check the squash growing outside
my small screened window.
This morning the lip of a leaf has curled
in longing towards its neighbor.
We can chart this growth,
half an inch a week, unlike my babies,
who wake one morning into childhood,
and just as suddenly demand I walk
two steps behind them.
I think of my friend, diagnosed with leukemia,
three children, pregnant with a fourth.
Illness has transformed her.
Her skin the grey-green of eucalyptus bark.
If I could transport her to my garden,
surround her with new growth -
The satsuma plum with its promising flowers,
the rampage of healthy ficus,
Her shoes would dissolve in the peat-laced moss.
Her feet would grow roots.

Anne F. Walker

Child's
(for D.L.V.)

During our pudding period, rather than blue
period, because we ate cups and cups of pudding while
cooking more to eat after and laughed that all artists
go through a kind of period like this pudding, rice pudding, period.

You told me that a scaly monster was in the closet and asked
if I was hungry. Scaly monsters love to be eaten.

You looked and it was still there but when I looked
it was gone. You found scaly monster footprints of mozzarella
and havarti fingerprints on the floor and walls toward the kitchen.
Asking me to lie in bed and wait, you found scaly monster eyes
just like peanut butter on French bread, with cream cheese irises
and raisin pupils

scattered on the kitchen counter,
one for you, and one for me.

George Elliot Clarke

Breakfast in Kingston
After Gwendolyn MacEwen

Your darkbrown hair, chestnut-falls,
rivers the pillow;
your lips pour into mine—
the taste of your French
sweet as Danish blue cheese.

We break open German coffee
and wild, stray bits of song,
crafting an early *noel*
of eggnog, cream of wheat
with cinnamon and something pink on top,
and cold cranberry juice.

Then we dine off cotton sheets,
you just wearing perfume;
my fingers reading you like the Bible.

The day disappears, and we feast in bed,
forgetting the grey wet snow of December.

We fall in love with a thousand things.

Lara Candland

Poetry

The baby's nails are smooth and short. Emanuelle feels like poetry. One nail is clipped too short. She goes to the cupboard and fishes for a band-aid. *Pitched past pitch of grief,* she remembers. But she does not know about grief, and she does not know where she got that line. She wants poetry. Something hard and old. *No worse there is none,* but that is not old enough.

She puts carrots through a strainer. The baby's mouth opens wide. After he eats his bowl of carrots, she puts him to her breast. The milk comes out fast. This makes her sleepy and she lies on the couch with Nicky and they both fall asleep.

Then Emanuelle hears music: while she sleeps there is a soundtrack, but what she really wants is poetry. *The poetry runs hard as sapp...* she is moving across the bay. She hears music and sees water and light and remembers the verses all wrong... *when I think how my light is used... when I think how my light is spent ...* Nicky stirs and Emanuelle thinks how she should get up and put the chicken in a pan. Nicky doesn't cry much and Jack isn't particular about dinner. She will just sprinkle some things on the chicken and stick it in the oven. She might clean the floor. The line she is searching for does not come. She does not fall asleep.

Later, she gets down on the floor and scrubs. Nicky still sleeps. His blood is thick like mine, his mother thinks, thick and slow, he likes to sleep, he has too much phlegm, he was born under Saturn. But these things are not all bad. The house smells like soap and chicken. Nicky is always happy.

"Are you a minimalist?" Jack says when he reads her poetry. She does not answer. My blood is thick, I am indecisive, she thinks, I am like Hamlet, my message is one of despair... *When in disgrace with fortune and men's eyes..* she likes to write poetry because it's short. The message is usually one of despair. My blood runs thick, cold, hard as sap, like poems, she thinks.

When Jack gets home he will like the smell of soap and chicken. Nicky will rise from his nap and be all warm and soft and sweet, smelling of milk.

She writes her stuff fast but it comes hard: it takes long to boil, it torments her and tears her apart. Often she forgets her great lines. The great ones are rare or non-existent.

"This is depressing," Jack says, "You're always so depressed." This is what he says when he reads her poetry. "But I like it," he adds.

Jack quotes lines she is unfamiliar with: *thou art summoned by sickness, Death's herald and champion.* They are manly lines: *I go back to Korea. Do I ever,* he says, *Do I ever.*

"I like your feet a lot," Jack says, "a lot." He touches them.

"Emanuelle," Jack says, "Where's this from? *It was not a very white jacket, but white enough . . .*"

"Are you asking me because you want to know, or is this a test?"

"Test," Jack says. They are eating little cups of pudding in bed.

"Melville," she says. They are living in New York now. Soon they will be living in Boston. Emanuelle feeds Jack spoonfuls of pudding. They are watching t.v. A man is wearing all black and pretending to be German. He is making fun of Germans.

They turn off the set and hear sirens and people using fireworks. They hear a car stereo. Nicky's little bed is in the front room and she gets up to feed him. Sometimes it takes a long time to nurse him because he is always looking at his mother and laughing.

Emanuelle checks the mirror on her way back to bed. She says her prayers. She snuggles up to Jack and falls asleep. Jack gets up early. When he leaves, she dreams of him. When she wakes, calls him on the phone. *By night on my bed I sought him whom my soul loveth: I sought him but I found him not,* she says to Jack over the phone.

She puts in a load of laundry and hangs all the whites out on the fire escape, then takes Nicky to the park where they sit on a bench and drink juice. They watch some boys playing basketball. A woman stops and pinches Nicky's cheek. "He's lovely," she says. "You should try olive oil on that," she points to a little rash on Nicky's face. Emanuelle holds back her hair while she speaks to the woman. She offers the woman a bagel because it seems like she is hungry. Nicky laughs at her and she touches his face again.

"My name is Miriam," the woman says.

"I'm Emanuelle."

"This is a very nice name," Miriam says. "Your mother has good taste."

Emanuelle laughs.

Miriam eats the bagel. Emanuelle offers her a banana. Miriam eats. They stop in a Middle Eastern shop for falafel and coffee. Miriam seems sleepy. Emanuelle invites her home for a shower and a bed.

While Miriam sleeps, Emanuelle cleans her oven. Nicky sits in his basket on the floor next to his mother. Miriam is wearing Emanuelle's nightie. Emanuelle scrubs the bathtub. She does not want Miriam to think she is a bad housekeeper. When the kitchen and bathroom are spotless, she organizes her desk and writes a note to her sister. She turns some very quiet music on the stereo and feeds Nicky. Nicky cries after he eats. His mother changes his diaper and pats his back until he burps. *Where did you find that little tear? I found it waiting when I got here. What makes your forehead so smooth and high? A soft hand stroked it as I went by.* Nicky and his mother nap on the couch. She dreams of the water again, a bay that is not Boston, a plane headed west, a sun she has never seen in New York.

While she sleeps, Miriam is in the kitchen chopping vegetables. When she wakes up, Miriam says, "If you run out for a little meat, I can make something delicious." So Emanuelle and Nicky go down to the butcher's and pick up some beef and buy a parsnip at Miriam's request. When they return they smell onions cooking. Miriam throws the beef in the pot, adds vegetables and paprika. Emanuelle opens a bottle of wine.

When it was not raining, a low mist moved across the paddies, blending the elements into a single grey element, and the war was cold and pasty and rotten. Jack said this to Emanuelle shortly after they first met. She had not been able to place it. She is too embarrassed to ask Jack where it came from now. Miriam's goulash simmers in the kitchen. Nicky and Miriam play on the couch. *Your father went to work,* Miriam sings, *he will return.* Nicky giggles. Emanuelle gives Miriam a sheaf of poems. Miriam reads while she plays with Nicky. Emanuelle holds a book that she is not reading.

"You think it is," Miriam says, "but your message is essentially *not* one of despair." Emanuelle closes her book. "I'm right," Miriam says, "trust me."

Jack should be home soon. *It was a bad time,* he once said. And it was. It had been a bad time then. "Who said this?" Jack once asked, *"The heart does not choose who it loves..."* Emanuelle did not answer. Who chooses? she thought.

Miriam continues to leaf through her poems. Emanuelle stands by the window, looking for Jack to come out of the subway. It is getting dark early now, and it rains lightly. She bounces Nicky on her hip. Miriam reads and reads. Jack does not appear as she waits by the window. *Saw ye him whom my soul loveth ...* Nicky falls asleep on his mother's shoulder... There is a moon out already... *The moon in its flight ...* Emanuelle thinks. She is tired of waiting. As she turns from the window, the moon, evanescent, fades behind a cloud. *I'd prefer not to think it was beauty on the wane.*

Damienne Grant Dibble

Beluga

Some folks like
their poetry straight out of the box it came in—
a silent read in a meditative hour, after midnight—
when life's buzz can be shushed
only by a laser-edged stare at some small human thing.

Some poet's eyes
can skin baloney
down to its original meat,
and somehow redress it
as beluga in a handmade tin.

Some midnight word snackers
will binge on such fare when they can get it,
but are otherwise content
with a can of Luck's beans, and a bottle of beer.

Brenda Hillman

Food

In a side booth at McDonald's before your music class
you go up and down in your seat like an arpeggio
under the poster of the talking hamburger:
two white eyes rolling around in the top bun, the thin
patty of beef imitating the tongue of its animal nature.
You eat merrily. I watch the Oakland mommies,
trying to understand what it means to be "single."

*

Across from us, females of all ages surround the birthday girl.
Her pale lace and insufficient being
can't keep them out of her circle.
Stripes of yellow and brown all over the place.
The poor in spirit have started to arrive,
the one with thick midwestern braids twisted like thought
on her head; ususally she brings her mother.
This week, no mother. She mouths her words anyway
across the table, space-mama, time-mama,
mama who should be there.

*

Families in line: imagine all this
translated by the cry of time moving through us,
this place a rubble. The gardens new generations
will plant in this spot, and the food will go on
in another order. This thought cheers me immensely.
That we will be there together, you still seven,
bending over the crops pretending to be royalty,

that the huge woman with one blind eye
and dots like eyes all over her dress
will also be there, eating with pleasure
as she eats now, right up to the tissue paper,
peeling it back like bright exotic petals.

*

Last year, on the sun-spilled deck in Marin
we ate grapes with the Russians;
the KGB man fingered them quickly and dutifully,
then, in a sad tone to us
"We must not eat them so fast,
we wait in line so long for these," he said.

*

The sight of food going into a woman's mouth
made Byron sick. Food is a metaphor for existence.
When Mr. Egotistical Sublime, eating the pasta,
poked one finger into his mouth, he made a sound.
For some, the curve of the bell pepper
seems sensual but it can worry you,
the slightly greasy feel of it.

*

The place I went with your father had an apartment to the left,
and in the window, twisted like a huge bowtie,
an old print bedspread. One day, when I looked over,
someone was watching us, a young girl.
The waiter had just brought the first thing:
an orange with an avocado sliced up CCCC
in an oil of forceful herbs. I couldn't eat it.
The girl's face stood for something

and from it, a little mindless daylight was reflected.
The businessmen at the next table
were getting off on each other and the young chardonnay.
Their briefcases leaned against their ankles.
I watched the young girl's face because for an instant
I had seen your face there,
unterrified, unhungry, and a little disdainful.
Then the waiter brought the food,
bands of black seared into it like the memory of a cage.

You smile over your burger, chattering brightly.
So often, at our sunny kitchen table,
hearing the mantra of the refrigerator,
I've thought there was nothing I could do but feed you;
and I've always loved the way you eat,
you eat selfishly, humming, bending
the french fries to your will, your brown eyes
spotting everything: the tall boy
who has come in with his mother, repressed rage
in espadrilles, and now carries the tray for her.
Oh this is fun, says the mother,
You stand there with mommy's purse.
And he stands there smiling after her,
holding all the patience in the world.

Deborah Artman

Woman With Child

The boy sleeps between her blades. He sleeps against her breath, his legs around her broadwaist, strapped to her back with cloth, sleeping. He dreams of water, he can smell the sea. It smells like fish, he is swimming. His head rocks with the water and only the land is still.

The woman kneels on the floor. She knows herself better with extra weight. She is preparing a meal—the slip of fish between her hands. She feels for an instant the thin life of the fish. Her hands rest on it calmly, owning it. The fish wakes up and flaps, all muscle. The boy beats his tiny fists against the back of his dream.

bpNichol

Fish/Wave

Bethlyn Madison Webster

Stamps

I'm watching the woman
who is watching my groceries
rolling along the conveyor belt.
She stands Cheerio-mouthed
in a pink and white dress
sporting a crisp, curled hairdo
and staring as much as she pleases
while I stand behind my husband,
hiding behind him and the baby.
She has seen him produce
a book of foodstamps
from his pocket, and I think she wants
to see how her tax dollars
are being wasted today.
Eggs, milk, peanut butter, bread
root beer and a bag of store brand
chocolate chips. She looks
at those the longest.
I want the tell her that we work
for ten cents above minimum.
I want to explain
that it's Friday, we're tired,
and our chocolate is none of her business.
Somehow, we're on display
along with the tabloids and gum.
With long pink-nailed fingertips,
she puts her stuff up now:
a big red rib-eye steak
a head of green lettuce,
the leafy kind, and a bottle of merlot.

Out total is rung
and my husband pays.
The checker lays the coupons upside-down,
like a blackjack hand,
and pounds them with a rubber stamp.

Lyn Lifshin

My Mother Wants Lamb Chops, Steaks, Lobster, Roast Beef

something to get
her teeth in
forget the shakes
cancer patients
are supposed to
choose forget
tapioca pudding
vanilla ice
she wants what
is full of blood
something to
chew to get the
the red color
out of something
she can attack
fiercely my
mother who never
was mamby-pamby
never held her
tongue never
didn't attack
or answer back
worry about
angering or hurt
ing anybody but
said what she
felt and wouldn't
walk any tight
rope, refuses the

pale and delicate
for what's blood
what she can
chew even spit
out if she
needs to

Walter Pavlich

All That Meat

Mostly gnawed half
chicken breast with a light
coating of diet red
spaghetti sauce slid into

the microwave to be
zonked for 150
seconds and then
eaten with a salad

fork the tines of the
devil in my mouth while
on TV for the umpteenth
time on the Andy

Griffith show Aunt Bea
betrays the town
butcher by buying
a side of beef from

a gimmicky new discount
shop   of course it turns
out the meat is tough and
her freezer goes kafunkus

on her so she asks her old
butcher would he store the
melting parcels of cow for her and he
says yes of course cause

she's been a good customer for
so long but Andy makes her take
all of it back home where he
has bought a new freezer at

full price but Bea scolds him for
not getting a better deal and I nod
at it all since there are lessons to
be learned all around on this one

for I have been butcher   Bea
fair and square Andy   hell I've
even been the meat   but don't you
forget they still have to eat all

that difficult beef so Bea will
hate herself everytime she thaws
out a package and Andy will
resent her when he picks the

gristle out of his teeth after
supper on the front porch while
Opie breathes in the smoke from Andy's
post-meal cigarette wondering about it all

John Gilgun

Clyde Steps In

The door of the truck stop opens and Clyde steps in. Fifteen feedcaps freeze in space. Fifteen upper lips pause at the chipped rims of fifteen coffee mugs. Thirty eyes slide sideways like nightcrawlers inching across a lawn. The talk had been about soybeans. Now there would be no more talk about soybeans. From a booth near the back, Mildred Haskins cries, "You can't carry one of them things in here!" Then nimbly and with incredible dexterity, Clyde raises the instrument of death and begins firing. Just before I hit the floor, I see a pat of butter melting on a hot blueberry muffin. A single crumb on the muffin materializes suddenly into the face of God. "This can't be happening!" I think. "After all, I've attended church every single Sunday of my life."

Susan Musgrave

Love Wasn't Always

You've been out back butchering
all week. I cleave the heart and fry
the last of the black boar in hog's grease
until his blood weeps. You like your piece
done so there's something for your teeth
to sink into. I watch you eat
and later, when you sleep, your body
smelling of jerked meat and the juice
that's been pent up in me all week,

I lie beside you thinking
love wasn't always this way with us.
"Ugly as love" you called the one sow
who wouldn't die quickly on the slab
the way you wanted her to, trusting you.

Love wasn't always this way. Sometimes
I thought it could last, like the first time
I came to you innocent as air

and you were waiting there.

Susan Ioannou

Synaesthesia

If the *squeak* of a polished apple
hooks the ear,
beef is a head of steam.
Thud hangs heavy as pork stew in a fog,
and *bump* gobs peanut butter.
Vinegar snarls in the throat like a rope,
but *rum* runs round as a mixing bowl.

Only *wood smoke* tastes like lost love.

Deborah Dashow Ruth

Grounds

Nothing but coffee traces
in the flowered cups
Her hand reaches for the one
beside the empty chair
She lifts that cup
turns it slowly
between both palms
until the still wet rim
meets her lips
inhales the faded
scent of French roast
then licks off
all that remains
of him

Marcia Lipson

Repast

Peering at the intravenous bag to check what's flowing into me,
I think of manna, and of hummingbirds
sipping nectar from the gullets of flowers
with a fervor I can't summon now,
so when I see the label reads Gonzalez,
I scream until the room fills with white coats
who hustle away my liquid feast, replacing it,
while trying to pacify me like a hummingbird
who's sustained by one red flower,
or another.

Bernadette Dyer

Kitchen Solitaire

Herbs abandoned hang from rafters on the ceiling,
Only silence lives there.
Blackened kettles and crusted pots
Wait in dank humidity
In corners where once I observed
Hot steam coiling from your soups and stews
While oil sputtered and sizzled in a frenzied dance
In the iron Dutch pot you so lovingly brought
Across the Nicaraguan border.

opal palmer adisa

Dinner Time

> *(for all the people of somalia and*
> *all people who are combating hunger)*

I

every day like clockwork
between 7 and 8 pm
i sit to dinner
with my children
there is at least one starch
two vegetables
one lean meat and often
several organically grown fruits
we drink bottled-water
and every day like clockwork
my three year old son
will spill as much as he eats
or throw food at his sister
across the table
my one year old
who is learning to feed herself
will offer more to the floor
than what gets in her stomach
my seven year old
will ask for seconds
and every day like clockwork
at the end of the meal
i will be satiated
often stuffed

when i clear the table
i will scrape food into a plastic bag
and though i often say to my children
who are always with food in their mouths
—snacks before meals
dessert after dinner—
don't waste food
people are starving
just in the park
near us
daily i will throw away food
knowing that
all over the world
many people are hungry

II

food is important
in my house
it always has been
even as a child
there was always much more than we could eat
my mother often left me sitting at the table
insisting that i eat up
she was more worried about me being thin
than wasting
she often remonstrated me with the same
words i offer to my children
"people are starving
don't waste food"
but i never ate up
and the dogs were
the happier for it

III

i can't imagine
my own child so thin
the breeze knocks her down
i can't envision my son
head and stomach bloated with air
i can't hold in my mind
my breasts so worn
only pus drips from them
i can't recognize my husband
bones sucking his skin
making him look like an aged
weather beaten twig

hunger is not where
i live
it never has been
hunger doesn't knock
on my door
if there was a disaster
any time
of the month or year
my family would have food in our cupboard
to eat three meals for
at least two weeks
hunger is not even a cousin
or a distant relative
hunger does not
stalk us

IV

but every day
like clockwork

for many
hunger is a constant
thirst is a constant
need is a constant
there is no "dinner time" call
children have no food
to toss across the room
or leave piled up in their plates
there are no seconds: "another leg please"
or choices: butter or catfish
no fruits: watermelon cantaloupe honeydew strawberry
no ice-cream cookies fig-bars
no canola oil low fat cholesterol free
no caffeine-free
no 100% natural no additives

nothing
except the vicious air
that blows the stench
of bodies devoured by hunger
just the sun
which saps the little energy
making the search more perilous
just the swarm of flies
that suck at the matter around
the eyes
and the scavengers perched
waiting for one more to fall
just the fingers numbed and caked with dirt
scratching at the earth
a little blood offering wetness
but no food
no drinking water
no bone

every day like clockwork
mothers place their stick-sized children
to their breast
hard and flat on their chests
every day like clockwork
men look away from the wife
whose skin once shone with life
and whose gait promised sweet memories
every day like clockwork
sons wander from their family
hoping to return
with a hand cupped with water
but every day like clockwork
they watch others succumb to hunger
they see hunger dancing in front of them
fully clothed and satisfied
and every day like clockwork
they will offer some of their own to hunger
who will not thank them then slink away shame-faced
but rather will remain bold   greedy
demanding more

V

we hear their plea
and offer what we can
but our gestures
are empty
not because we are insincere
but it doesn't stop us
from eating wasting
being satisfied
our sincerity doesn't stop
their hunger
not forever

not even for a year
we forget
claiming we must continue
we turn our heads
from the devastation
we do not stop
to figure out
how to redirect the course of water
stop the civil war
re-fertilize the land
something permanent   lasting
because every day like clockwork
most of us here will eat
at least one meal
will be satisfied
will know that tomorrow
there will be another meal
so the sight of hunger
does not stop our excess
does not stop our indulgence
does not stop us from eating
every day
like clockwork
everyday
like clock work
americans consume themselves
numb

Mary di Michele

Hunger in the Text

The reason the poet writes is to fill in the blank   sky. Those infinite fields of   emptiness in the map of the universe. Milky Way lite is not a reduced-calorie chocolate bar but   that trickle of stars in the immense

of nothing. Stellar spaces began to intrude into poetry in the lines of Mallarme. He followed the crisis in the poem to the urban grid where all the streets ended   somewhere. In snacks and shopping. I tried to feed him there in Montreal, in Cathedral Mall, treating him to lunch at McDonald's. In the light of neon arches, there is no unleased space. In the light of neon arches, there is no

nourishment. Allons-y mon ami! Let's go by a throw of the dice or those coins for the I Ching. We just missed it, the universe, for popcorn and the last picture show at the cineplex. Then matters grew worse when I lost my mentor in the crush of the midnight madness sale. Time

to go home. The poet travels by metro. She enters the last car so that she may again watch, through the window and into the blackest tunnel, as the jetsam of crumpled chip bags and candy wrappers, as the world of hungry things flies off . . .

bpNichol

The Tonsils

1.

They said 'you don't need them' but they were keen to cut them out. They said 'if they swell up they'll choke you to death' so you learned they cut things off if they might swell up. There were two of them in their sacs & they hung there in your throat. They cut them off.

2.

I didn't have them long enough to grow attached to them but they were attached to me. It was my first real lesson in having no choice. It was my only time ever in a hospital as a kid & I wasn't even sick. I wasn't even sick but I had the operation. I had the operation that I didn't want & I didn't day 'no' because there was no choice really. I had everybody who was bigger than me telling me this thing was going to happen & me crying a lot & them telling me it was good for me. It was my first real lesson in having no attachments.

3.

Almost everyone I knew had their tonsils out. Almost everyone I knew was told 'it's good for you.' Even tho none of us who had our tonsils out ever knew any kid who choked to death from having them in, almost everyone we knew had their tonsils out.

4.

I miss my tonsils. I think my throat used to feel fuller. Now my throat feels empty a lot & maybe that's why I eat too fast filling the throat with as much as I can. Except food is no substitute for tonsils. The throat just gets empty again.

5.

I was told I didn't need my tonsils. Maybe this is the way it is. Maybe as you grow older they tell you there are other bits you don't need & they cut them out. Maybe they just like cutting them out. Maybe tonsils are a delicacy doctors eat & the younger they are the sweeter. Maybe this is just paranoia. I bet if I had a lobotomy they could cut this paranoia out.

6.

What cutting remarks! What rapier wit! What telling thrusts! Ah cut it out! Cut it short! He can't cut it! You said a mouthful!

7.

There are two of them & they hang there in your throat. There are two of them in sacs & they swell up. Now there are none. Gosh these words seem empty!

Andrea Adolph

Under an Arbor I Imagine Your Vegetables

Peppers charred ebony
and peeled back, exposed
flesh red and soft as ever—
these are your palette,
the water-filled, the jewel-like,
this sweet skin
and the nubbed
green of peas, butternut
squash giving way
to the tongue, summer's
yellow tomatoes plunged
into a roiling kettle, scalded
as if in punishment.

Venantius Fortunatus

Gogo

> *translated by Geoffrey Cook*

Nectar
> wine
>> bread
>>> raiment
>>>> discourse
>>>>> abundance

You entertain me liberally:
> Gogo:
>> you are an ebbing Cicero
>> our feasting Apicus.

You plant with words
> then, you tend with food.
But, pardon me!
> I rest
>> swollen with beef
>>> my embroiled flesh rumbles
>>> my belly quarrels.
This, I know
> the chicken & goose avoid a reclining ox
>> for it would be insane to fight horns with feathers
&, now, I confine/my drooping eyes/in dream
> My sluggish verses recommend me/for sleep.

Anne F. Walker

Peach Offering

Sliver moon
sets into an orange horizon
in less time than it takes
to smoke half a cigarette in blue fading light.

A seagull flickers white across like limned by smokestacks
city   turquoise

water
a mirror for scads of delicate turning sky.

You have a magic illness
and when you wake
from it   you will see and feel
things you haven't
since you were very
young and clear.

And this peach
sweet enough to tie a light to your lips.

Katie Kingston

Phoung

Against the sage backdrop
Phoung straightens damp sheets
along a piece of sailing rope.
The jeans of her Amerasian daughters
hang in sequence on the chain links.
When the wind lifts a pair
to my lawn, we talk about the coolness
in these late mornings.

She bends to gather leaves
at her ankles, holds them to me
for names. These sprigs, broken to air,
hold their breath against mine, "cilantro,"
a wave of what is foreign. Today
we will learn this recipe, old
from her mother, a blending
with soy noodles, black mushrooms.

Rubbing the wok with warmed oil
to preserve the rusted metal, she begins
this stir fry with ginger root sauces.
Between sips of Oolong, she tells
about this other life, in Saigon,
where she met this American husband,
how they stored their drinking water
in empty vodka bottles.

She moves to the cutting board.
Breaking the banded celery, slicing
the stalks as if they were bok choy,

she tells of her mother who surfaced
thorugh the black market two months
before. How we gathered the children
in front of the polaroid, hoping
this underground could find her

one more time. Pulling the skin
from jicama, its old name
under her breath, she lines it
with the cleaver. The blade cuts
its sharpness into wood, presses
coldness to her fingers, menaces,
yet never quite touches.

Dave Kelly

Use a Fork, Not a Blender, to Mix the Guacamole
For Donna Carradine and Frank Lima

Eating Mexican food always makes me think of my favorite Tony Quinn movie. A beautiful movie, filled with violence and corruption and the terribleness of being virile and fifty. Tony Quinn plays all the parts except the female lead, and that is the woman who once was married either to Marlon Brando or to John Wayne or Ernest Borgnine. No, I don't mean Ethel Merman.

It goes something like this: when I eat tacos, the kind you get at drive-in restaurants, I sometimes think of Marlon Brando in Viva Zapata, especially at the end, where the flies are swarming around his "bullet-riddled body"; when I add hot sauce to the tacos, I may even think of Gilbert Roland, remember? with the wrist bands and those great black cigarillos?

But when I'm sitting over a huge bowl of menudo, with a fistful of raw onions swimming among the tripes and beans, or when I spoon a hot salsa ranchera over a plate of enchiladas, it's got to be Quinn, tough and wretched, with that beautiful woman loving him a little, despising him a little, a little afraid of him.

Marlene Goldman

For Mitchel

Carrying parcels—meat, bread, the bottle of wine—
chilvary loses to gravity.
You catch two bags against your knees;
the third falls.

Liquid gathers round your socks.

The moment hangs in the air for days.

Sheri Radford

Outline

under her fingernails, pasta bits catch
as she scrubs and scrubs
hard spaghetti sauce off plates
remnants of her Valentine's day

dinner was the gift she gave
a messy kitchen was the gift she received

she rubs a soapy finger on her itchy nose
then scrubs and scrubs at the plates

she can make out traces of dinner on the floor
splatters of sauce

if she chalked an outline around the splatters
they'd almost form a person
a complete person
who would have bought gifts and roses
and heart-shaped boxes of chocolates

Sylvia Legris

quartet
of banana desserts:

bananas caribbean
banana souffles
ambrosia cake (symmetrical garnish of tangerine wedges, banana slices)
tea bread (spread with sweet butter)

when i was 13 went on my first diet
the doctor told me to avoid bananas
all starch she said

sometimes at safeway i peel blue chiquita stickers
off bananas stick them to my fridge door (sometimes
i walk around safeway with
chiquita sticker eyelids amazing
what people don't notice even when i smile
bat my lashes)

amazing

Maureen Hynes

Inedible

Certain Guiness records, the gruesome
ones, are gnawing at me,
the man who ate a bus, for example,
and what got him going (his plastic
soldiers, the rubber wheels
on his sister's doll carriage
the caboose of his own train set)
who encouraged him and
is he okay now? On those pages
there are no consequences,
no lacerated innards or curdled bones
or iron filings in his tears.

I remember the last meal she made me
her five o'clock panic set off
by fifty years of dinner rituals
she elbowed me away from the stove
pierced the kitchen with the shriek
of the kettle and the pressure cooker
laid the table with alacrity

six settings in good china and family silver
for the two of us
my old pink cereal bowl full of stumpy-chopped raw onions
a stack of packaged cookies, hard disks on a plate
a saucer of wrinkled peas, the peas
choking in melted margarine
aluminum pitcher of milk

the bowl of boiled potatoes
and a pot of tea
were the things she could still get right

at first that haywire meal was angry tinfoil
in my throat, inedible

but once swallowed, ambered
into a resinous rational lump

Patty Seyburn

Ritual

At the Passover table,
my grandma refuses
to recline, as the holiday
mandates. She eats
parsley we leave
on our plates, first
dousing it in salt water,
squinting her pale, blue
eyes at the tang. Her hardboiled
egg thoroughly peppered,
she bites into the white
and yellow crescent, chewing
slowly as a gourmand
who can't quite place
some recondite spice.
She buys white horseradish
no one else can
bear and slathers it
on matzah. "I can only
taste hot," she says,
answering a question
no one has asked for
decades, her tastebuds
inured to mild or sweet.
Over and over, she
burns her own tongue.

Joan Jobe Smith

Hot and Hungry

All of her life my mother would
be hot and hungry because of
the years she spent when a little
girl picking cotton in hot, dusty
Texas, picking and waiting for
the dinnerbell, picking and waiting
for the little colored gal with the
waterbucket to come down her row
the bucket always full of bugs
my mother hated and would later
when a tidy wife chase crazy
assassin from her clean house
and she would become a waitress
to be near the food, the foaming
root beer floats, icy Coca Colas,
sizzling hamburgers and t-bones.

I always thought she was lucky
when I was a kid, thought picking
cotton, walking in the sun all
day, seemed like play until we
went to my Uncle Euen's farm in
Denton and my cousin Jake showed
me their cotton field, the stickery
bulbs of white, dry-bone stuff, showed
me how to pick the coarse core that
made my fingertips crack and sting
sore after only ten picks and he
laughed at my city slickerness
while I got hot and hungry and

wished my mother could've been like
me and made mudpies beneath summer
shade trees, waiting for the ice
cream man on his way down the street.

Jeff Mann

Serviceberry

Serviceberry derived its name from the time of its blooming: about the time mountain thaws could allow the circuit preacher to reach remote areas and hold services for those who had died during the winter.

Soils blush in green, a faint
renaissance across pastures,
these gambol-weeks of Angus calves.
Along riverbanks, an emerald whispering
begins. Above, the sky still shivers
winter, the Alleghanies are rainy veilings,
smoke billows, pewter depthlessness.

Against that gloom, serviceberry
blooms, as if ghosts were beckoning,
snow were snagged, or antique lace
tattered on twig tips.

Ectoplasms of the mountain dead,
these petals. Kin interred in
winter without observance,
far from hearth-red crumblings,
quilt-heaped loving, bereft
of biscuit dough, early rhubarb,
coffee and fresh calvings.

The gnarled roads are open now,
the circuit preacher comes.
Revenants want remembrance, all the blooming
they have missed, a circle of service,
bent heads, as serviceberry spumes

about raw hilltop mounds, as pieced sod
revives above boxes denied the thaw.

Christopher Woods

Potatoes By Phone

Reading it the third time,
I am still amazed.
Hungry, after midnight,
In a hotel room in Galveston,
I scan the room service menu in my lap.
There under the "Omelette" heading,
It says all are served with warm biscuits
And yes, with "mourning" potatoes.

I am a realist and do not believe
That biscuits will climb four floors
And arrive still warm at my door.
That they arrive at all is sufficient.
That I have lived all this time,
Through all kinds of culinary weather,
Never to know that some potatoes,
By design or scheme or recipe,
Are meant only for mourning.
I have eaten them in all kinds of moods,
Even outside my homeland,
Never once, I think, funereally.

But I am also starving.
I pick up the phone and dial,
Ordering them without question.
Then, waiting in the dark,
I hear waves crash against the seawall.
Somewhere in the bowels of this old hotel
A cart is rolling this way,
And for an instant

I do not care if even death
Comes riding on it.

Diane Glancy

Generally he gave them plenty of room

The Audubon Society sells seeds in winter. Niger thistle, cracked corn, millet, sunflower, manna suet cakes, for whatever flies. Finches, quail, blackbirds. Whenever the wild sky smoke-signals the morning. The men talk about the Indians who used to drive to Pawhuska and walk up Main Street. Buffalo robes and horns on the hood of their car. Sometimes running out of gas, they walked away and left it there. *Generally he gave them plenty of room*, the man says. They wrapped in blankets in those days. Wore moccasins and feathers. A sack of seed would feed 20 Osage, but Cherokees farmed their corn until old and sick they stopped their growing and ate like birds.

Patience Wheatley

Bird's Nest Soup

"Draw it." I say
when he asks what I'll do with
this small nest
just 2 inches across
like a miniature
grey wig
or upside down
duchess' hat from
Alice in Wonderland,

these strands of plastic
glinting alongside grass
soft kleenex shreds, dryer-fluff
cat-fur and the odd bit of
chewed paper for structural strength
and mud

"What will you do with it?" he asks me again

afraid I'll keep it, thinking of
bird shit
bugs or worse.

My pan's at the simmer
recipes bubbling
senses kindled

"Cook it," I say.

Bethlyn Madison Webster

Dove Season

The doveshot frightened the horses when it came
down like hail on the tin roof of the stable.
It startled the buckskin to dance around and rear,
but I rode bareback through air sweet with clover,
my horse shying at gunshots, his thick skin
quivering. Across the neighbor's field,
shirtless boys with dogs and shouldered guns
wiped their sweat and waved as we rushed by.
The men were at their homemade grill—
a split oil-barrel covered with mesh.
One had a knife, the other a brush,
and he basted bite-size pieces of flesh.
A mound still pink covered a paper plate.
One man handed me a cup of iced-tea
and asked me to stay for dinner.
But I couldn't get the horse to stop
shying away from the bushel of birds
with their eyes tiny slits and their breasts cut out.

Michael D. Riley

Beast Fable

He knows only footprints in the snow,
reflections just above the rim
passing like the shadow
of a cloud over playground or pool,
the distance between muscle and mind
where he traps his likeness,
his elbow a cocked trigger,
fingers aiming to grasp and seize,
steadying self-hate on its journey
past the cross-hair hours,
drawing down on him old sinew and nerve,
veins of habit all along the skin
where the pores gap, gun barrels
freezing the emptied face,
still almost expressionless
except for the separating lips,
their edges curling slightly upward.

Beverley A. Brenna

Farm Woman Displaced

She dreams of gardens
like a pregnant woman craves pickles.
Green and fresh
she sees them stretching toward her,
smells their dewy skin.

When she wakes
she stumbles to the fridge,
forgetting what she wants
but driven   something.

Her mouth filled with cheese and bread,
she rocks against the shelf,
unsatisfied.
All she tastes is dust.

Margaret Atwood

Bread

Imagine a piece of bread. You don't have to imagine it, it's right here in the kitchen, on the bread board, in its plastic bag, lying beside the bread knife. The bread knife is an old one you picked up at an auction; it has the word BREAD carved into the wooden handle. You open the bag, pull back the wrapper, cut yourself a slice. You put butter on it then peanut butter, then honey, and you fold it over. Some of the honey runs out onto your fingers and you lick it off. It takes you about a minute to eat the bread. This bread happens to be brown, but there is also white bread, in the refrigerator, and a heel of rye you got last week, round as a full stomach then, now going mouldy. Occasionally you make bread. You think of it as something relaxing to do with your hands.

*

Imagine a famine. Now imagine a piece of bread. Both of these things are real but you happen to be in the same room with only one of them. Put yourself into a different room, that's what the mind is for. You are now lying on a thin mattress in a hot room. The walls are made of dried earth and your sister, who is younger than you are, is in the room with you. She is starving, her belly is bloated, flies land on her eyes; you brush them off with your hand. You have a cloth too, filthy but damp, and you press it to her lips and forehead. The piece of bread is the bread you've been saving, for days it seems. You are as hungry as she is, but not yet as weak. How long does this take? When will someone come with more bread? You think of going out to see if you might find something that could be eaten, but outside the streets are infested with scavengers and the stink of corpses is everywhere.

Should you share the bread or give the whole piece to your sister? Should you eat the piece of bread yourself? After all, you have a better chance of living, you're stronger. How long does it take to decide?

*

Imagine a prison. There is something you know that you have not yet told. Those in control of the prison know that you know. So do those not in control. If you tell, thirty or forty or a hundred of your friends, your comrades, will be caught and will die. If you refuse to tell, tonight will be like last night. They always choose the night. You don't think about the night, however, but about the piece of bread they offered you. How long does it take? The piece of bread was brown and fresh and reminded you of sunlight falling across a wooden floor. It reminded you of a bowl, a yellow bowl that was once in your home. It held apples and pears; it stood on a table you can also remember. It's not the hunger or the pain that is killing you but the absence of the yellow bowl. If you could only hold the bowl in your hands, right here, you could withstand anything, you tell yourself. The bread they offered you is subversive, it's treacherous, it does not mean life.

*

There were once two sisters. One was rich and had no children, the other had five children and was a widow, so poor that she no longer had any food left. She went to her sister and asked her for a mouthful of bread. 'My children are dying,' she said. The rich sister said, 'I do not have enough for myself,' and drove her away from the door. Then the husband of the rich sister came home and wanted to cut himself a piece of bread; but when he made the first cut, out flowed red blood.

Everyone knew what that meant.

This is a traditional German fairy-tale.

*

The loaf of bread I have conjured for you floats about a foot above your kitchen table. The table is normal, there are no trap doors in it. A blue tea towel floats beneath the bread, and there are no strings attaching the cloth to the bread or the bread to the ceiling or the table to the cloth, you've proved it by passing your hand above and below. You didn't touch the bread though. What stopped you? You don't want to know whether the bread is real or whether it's just a hallucination I've somehow duped you into seeing. There's no doubt that you can see the bread, you can even smell it, it smells like yeast, and it looks solid enough, solid as your own arm. But can you trust it? Can you eat it? You don't want to know, imagine that.

CONTRIBUTOR NOTES

opal palmer adisa is the Chair of Ethnic Studies at the California College of Arts and Crafts. Her most recent book is *Tamarind and Mango Women* (Sister Vision Press, 1992).

Andrea Adolph has appeared in numerous literary journals including *Cimarron Review* and *Poetry Flash*. She holds a MFA in Creative Writing from Mills College and *Improv* (Redwood Coven Press, 1994) is her most recent book.

Deborah Artman has received fellowships from the MacDowell Colony, the Provincetown Fine Arts Work Center and the Ludwig Vogelstein Foundation. Her work has appeared in *The Carolina Quarterly*, *The Seattle Review*, and *Cottonwood Review*.

Margaret Atwood, best-selling author and Toronto artist, is one of the major forces bringing Canadian literature into the world arena. In 1994 she was knighted in France for her literary accomplishments. *The Robber Bride* (1994) is her most recent book.

Beryl Baigent has eight published books. Her most recent is entitled *Hiraeth: In Search of Celtic Origins* (Third Eye Publications, 1994).

John D. Bargowski, Sr. is a recent graduate of Lehigh University. He has published poetry in several journals including *Red Dancefloor* and *Slipstream*.

Anne Barney has published in *The Christian Science Monitor* and *Chiron Review*. Her most recent collection of poetry and prose is *Stolen Joy: Healing After Infertility and Infant Loss* (Icarus Books, 1993).

Chana Bloch is the Director of the Creative Writing Program at Mills College and an NEA grant recipient for translation. Her new translation of the biblical *Song of Songs*, in collaboration with Ariel

Bloch, has just been published by Random House.

Beverley A. Brenna is a freelance writer and children's storyteller who has published articles in newspapers, magazines and journals in Canada, the US and Britain. She holds a Master's degree in Education.

Susan Bumps holds a MFA in Creative Writing from Mills College. Her poetry has appeared in the *Santa Barbara Review* and *Art/Life*.

Lara Candland is the poetry editor for *hip mama*. Her work has appeared in numerous journals and she holds a MFA in Creative Writing from Mills College.

Kelly Cherry is the author of fourteen books and Evjue-Bascom Professor at the University of Wisconsin, Madison. Her first book of poems, *Lovers and Agnostics*, is soon to be reprinted through the Carnegie Mellon University Press.

George Elliot Clarke is a Professor of Canadian and African-American literature at Duke University. His most recent book of poetry is *Lush Dreams, Blue Exile* (1994).

Donia Blumenfeld Clenman was awarded an honorary degree of Doctor of Literature for "distinguished achievement in poetry" by the World Academy of Arts and Culture in 1994.

Geoffrey Cook is the author of *A Basket of Chestnuts: From the Miscellanea of Venantius Fortunatus* (Cherry Valley Editions, 1981), a book of translations. He lives in Berkeley, California.

Barbara Crooker is the author of six books and an NEA grant recipient. Her new book, *Moving Poems* is forthcoming through Camel Press.

Lorna Crozier won Canada's highest literary honour, the Governor General's Award, in 1992. She teaches at the University of Victoria and her new book, *Everything Arrives at the Light*, is forthcoming from McClelland & Stewart.

Mary di Michele teaches at Concordia University in Montreal. Her most recent collection is *Luminous Emergencies* (McClelland & Stewart, 1992). Her current work-in-progress is *Debriefing the Rose.*

Alphonse Daudet (1840-1897) gained a reputation in the latter half of the nineteenth century as a chronicler of the south of France and Provençe.

Carol V. Davis is a writer and translator whose work has appeared in such journals as *Mid-American Review* and *Tikkun*. Her recent chapbook is entitled *Letters From Prague* (Paper Bag Press, 1991.)

Damienne Grant Dibble is a writer and editor living in West Virginia. A chapbook of her poems, *Mudsuck Rap and other poems*, will be available in Spring of 1995.

Rachel Blau DuPlessis is the director of Temple University's Creative Writing Program. *Draft X: Letters* (Singing Horse Press, 1991) is her recent poetry collection from which "T" is excerpted.

Bernadette Dyer is a writer, illustrator, and storyteller whose work has appeared on CBC. She has performed at Toronto's Harbourfront and published in numerous journals and anthologies.

Maureen Eppstein lives in Palo Alto, California. Her poems have appeared in many journals including *Blue Unicorn* and *Kalliope*.

Christine Erwin is an Ontario poet whose work has appeared in several journals including *Grain* and *Quarry.*

Kathleen Evans is a writer and teacher living in Santa Cruz, California. She has had several poems published in small literary magazines.

Elizabeth Follin-Jones has appeared in several publications including *The Washington Post* and *The Pennsylvania Review*. Her poetry chapbook, *One Flight From The Bottom*, won the 1990 Artscape Literary Arts Award.

Bishop Venantius Fortunatus was born in Trieste in 530 in what was left of the Roman Empire in the West. "Gogo" originates from his travels through Gaul. He died in 610.

Diane Glancy received her MFA from the University of Iowa. Her seventh book, *Monkey Secret*, will be published this year by TriQuarterly/Northwestern University Press.

John Gilgun teaches at Missouri Western State College. His most recent book is *From the Inside Out* (Three Phase, 1991).

Marlene Goldman teaches at the University of Toronto. She has published in numerous journals including *Rampike* and *Canadian Literature*.

Vidas Gvozdzius has published previously in *Writers' Forum* and *Painted Hills Review*.

Claire Harris co-editor of *Kitchen Talk* (Red Deer College Press, 1992). *Drawing Down a Daughter* (Goose Lane Editions, 1991) is her recent poetry collection from which "Child   This is the Gospel on Bakes" is excerpted.

Barbara A. Hendryson is a native San Franciscan whose poetry has appeared in many journals including *Calyx* and the *Berkeley Poetry Review*.

Marie Henry has had her poetry appear in numerous journals and anthologies including *Yellow Silk* and *Only Morning in Her Shoes* (Utah State U.P.).

Brenda Hillman was short-listed for the 1994 Pulitzer Prize for her most recent book of poetry, *Bright Existence* (Wesleyan U.P., 1993). She is a 1994 Guggenheim Fellow, an NEA grant recipient, and a Professor at St. Mary's College in California.

Maureen Hynes has published poetry in many journals including *The Malahat Review* and *Poetry Canada*. Her book of poetry, *Rough Skin*, is forthcoming from Wolsak & Wynn in 1995.

Susan Ioannou is the author of *Clarity Between Clouds: Poems of Midlife* (Goose Lane Edition, 1991). Her work has appeared in numerous journals such as *The Malahat Review* and *Toronto Life*.

Sarah Gail Johnson is a student at the University of Wisconsin, Madison

Dave Kelly is a poet living in Geneseo, N.Y

Katie Kingston has been previously published in several literary magazines including *Ellipsis* and *Hawai'i Review*.

Melody Lacina has had work appear in *Berkeley Poetry Review* and *Rain City Review*. She has poetry forthcoming in the *Bellingham Review*.

John B. Lee is the author of many poetry collections. His most recent is *These Are The Days of Dogs And Horses* (Black Moss Press, 1994).

Sylvia Legris has published recently in many journals including *Prairie Fire* and *Contemporary Verse 2*. Her chapbook, *pathological lies (and other disorders)*, is just out through Moonprint Press.

Lyn Lifshin has edited many books of women's writing including *Adriane's Thread* (Harper and Row) and *Tangled Vine* (Beacon Press). *Blue Tattoo* (Event Horizon Press, 1995) is her most recent, of many, books.

Marcia Lipson teaches at Hunter College. Her work has most recently appeared in *The Plum Review* and *Kerem.*

Jeff Mann lives in Blacksburg VA and teaches at Virginia Tech. His poems have appeared in many magazines including *Iris* and *The Laurel Review.*

Elise M. McClellan recently read on the Acadiana Open Channel in Lafayette LA. This reading was met with both dismay and scandalous approval.

Seymour Mayne has had his work collected in some 35 books, chapbooks, and broadsides. His recent book, *Killing Time* (1992) was awarded the Jewish Book Committee Prize.

Wesley McNair has received, among others, Guggenheim and NEA Fellowships. His recent book is entitled *My Brother Running.*

Sandra McPherson is a Professor of English at the University of California, Davis. Her most recent of nine books is *The God Of Indeterminacy*(University of Illinois Press, 1993).

Sheila Meads has published in several journals including *Grain* and *Secrets from the Orange Couch*. In 1994 one of her stories was nominated by *Pottersfield Portfolio* for the Journey Prize.

Scott Minar has had writing appear in many journals including *The Georgia Review* and *Prisminternational.*

Felicia Mitchell has had her poetry published in a variety of journals and anthologies. She is the author of *Words & Quilts: A Selection of Quilt Poems.*

Hayley R. Mitchell is co-founder and editor of *Sheila-na-gig.* Her work is forthcoming in several journals including *Pearl* and *California Poetry Quarterly.*

Patricia Monaghan is the author of three books of non-fiction and two books of poetry, *Winterburning* and *Seasons of the Witch.*

Susan Musgrave is the Writer in Residence at the University of Toronto for 1995. Her most recent book is entitled *Forcing the Narcissus* (McClelland and Stewart, 1994).

bpNichol, always a friend of small presses and independent thinkers, won Canada's highest literary honour, the Governor General's Award, in 1970 for his achievement in four different volumes published that year. His recent book, *An H in the Heart,* (McClelland and Stewart, 1994) was published posthumously.

Alden Nowlan (1933-1983) was the author of 22 books of poetry, fiction and non-fiction. His selected work appears in *An Exchange of Gifts* (Irwin Publishing, 1985).

David Oates performs at poetry 'slams,' other readings, and belongs to a poetry and comedy performance group "Things You Need to Hear." His recent book is entitled *Night of the Potato* (Sow's Ear Press).

Diana O'Hehir has been nominated for a Pulitzer Prize. Her most recent book is *Home Free* (Atheneum, 1988) and she edited *Mother Songs* (W.W. Norton & Co., 1995) with Sandra Gilbert and Susan Gubar.

Michael Ondaatje, celebrated author and Toronto artist, is one of the major forces bringing Canadian literature into the world arena. He has won the UK's highest literary award, the Booker Prize, for his recent book, *The English Patient.*

Linda Pastan is Poet Laureate for Maryland. She is the author of more than seven books including the recent *Heroes in Disguise* (W.W. Norton & Co., 1991).

Walter Pavlich has published in numerous journals and anthologies. *Running near the End of the World* (University of Iowa Press, 1991) is his recent book of poetry.

Sheri Radford is an English and Creative Writing student at the University of Victoria. She has previously published in several journals including *American Goat* and *Bohemian Chronicle.*

Michael D. Riley, a Professor of English the Pennsylvania State University, has had his poetry published in numerous journals including *Poetry* and *Poetry Ireland Review.* His recent poetry collection is entitled *Mortal Blessings.*

Deborah Dashow Ruth has had poetry appear in journals such as *Zyzzyva* and *Poetpourri.*

M. Carmen Santos is a graduate of Skidmore College in, New York and is currently in the M. F. A. program at the University of Alaska.

Lawrence Schimel has published in various journals and anthologies including *The Saturday Evening Post* and *Sun Dog.* He lives in Manhattan.

Patty Seyburn earned her MFA in Creative Writing at the University of California, Irvine. Her work has appeared in many journals including *The New York Quarterly* and *Pearl.*

Joan Jobe Smith is founding editor of the literary journal *Pearl*. Her eighth collection of poetry, *Trying On Their Souls For Size* (The Poetry Business, 1994) was published in Great Britain.

Rosemary Sullivan is a Professor at the University of Toronto and a 1994 Guggenheim Fellow. Her most recent book of poetry is *Blue Panic* (Black Moss Press, 1991).

Heather Spears won Canada's highest literary honour, the Governor General's Award, for *The Word for Sand* (Wolsak & Wynn, 1989). She lives in Copenhagen and has published three books of drawings, three novels and nine collections of poetry.

Donald L. Vallis is currently researching early and mediaeval literature at the University of California, Berkeley. He won a National Film Board award for his film, *A Kid From the Suburbs*, a portrait of one man's struggle with terminal illness.

Ronald Wallace directs the Creative Writing Program at the University of Wisconsin, Madison. *Time's Fancy* (University of Pittsburgh Press, 1994) is his most recent of nine books.

Anne F. Walker, a Toronto based artist, is currently researching cultural impressions in poetic space at the University of California, Berkeley. Her third book of poetry, *Into the Peculiar Dark*, is forthcoming from Coach House Press in the Fall of 1995.

Ioanna-Veronika Warwick has published in many journals including *Poetry* and *Ploughshares*. She lives and writes in Chula Vista, California.

Bethlyn Madison Webster lives and writes in Fresno, California.

J. Weintraub is a Chicago writer who has published widely in such journals as *Kansas Quarterly* and *Cream City Review*.

Leonore Wilson teaches Creative Writing at Napa Valley College. She has published in numerous journals including *California Quarterly* and *Yellow Silk*.

Patience Wheatley has published in many journals including the Canadian Women Writers' Issue of *Prairie Schooner*. *Good-bye to the Sugar Refinery* (Goose Lane Editions, 1989) is her most recent book.

Edward Wolf has had work appear in many journals including *Transfer 36* and *New Writing from Gay and Lesbian San Francisco*. He is currently working on a book about the AIDS epidemic entitled *One Life, One Death*.

Christopher Woods is the author of *The Dream Patch,* a lyrical novel about a Texas family in the 1940's. His plays have been produced in Houston, Chicago, Atlanta, Los Angeles and New York City.

ACKNOWLEDGMENTS

OPAL PALMER ADISA Poetry printed by permission of author.
ANDREA ADOLPH "Someone Had to Eat It" from *Jubal.* "Salt
Eater" from *Improv* (Redwood Coven Press). Poetry printed by
permission of author. DEBORAH ARTMAN Poetry printed by
permission of author. MARGARET ATWOOD "Late August" from
You Are Happy (Oxford University Press) and *Selected Poems 1965-
1975* (Oxford University Press). "Bread" from *Murder in the Dark*
(Coach House Press). Poetry reprinted by permission of the author.
BERYL BAIGENT "Chernobyl Summer" from *Absorbing the Dark*
(Moonstone Press). Poetry printed by permission of the author.
JOHN D. BARGOWSKI, SR. Poetry printed by permission of the
author. ANNE BARNEY Poetry printed by permission of the
author. CHANA BLOCH "Eating Babies" from *The Past Keeps
Changing* (Sheep Meadow Press). Poetry printed by permission of
the author. BEVERLEY A. BRENNA "Farm Woman Displaced"
from *Harvest.* Poetry printed by permission of the author. SUSAN
BUMPS "Giving Homage to the Summer Fruit God" from *Santa
Barbara Review.* Poetry printed by permission of the author. LARA
CANDLAND Prose printed by permission of the author. KELLY
CHERRY "Woman Living Alone" reprinted by permission of
Louisiana State University Press from *God's Loud Hand* by Kelly
Cherry. © 1974, 1975, 1976, 1977, 1979, 1980, 1983, 1985, 1987, 1988,
1989, 1990, 1991, 1992, 1993 by Kelly Cherry. "Lunch at the Lake"
reprinted from *Cumberland Poetry Review.* "Lt. Col. Valentina
Vladimirovna Tereshkova" reprinted from *Relativity*, Louisiana State
University Press, by permission of the author. GEORGE ELLIOT
CLARKE Poetry printed by permission of the author. DONIA
BLUMENFELD CLENMAN Poetry printed by permission of the
author. GEOFFREY COOK translating VENANTIUS FORTUNATUS
"Gogo" from *A Basket of Chestnuts: From the Miscellanea of Venatius
Fortunatus* (Cherry Valley Editions). Poetry translation printed by
permission of the translator. BARBARA CROOKER "Picking Sour
Pie Cherries" from *Starting From Zero* (Great Elm Press). Poetry

185 I bite to eat place

Poetry printed by permission of the author. SARAH GAIL JOHNSON Poetry printed by permission of the author. DAVE KELLY Poetry printed by permission of the author. KATIE KINGSTON Poetry printed by permission of the author. MELODY LACINA Poetry printed by permission of the author. JOHN B. LEE Poetry printed by permission of the author. SYLVIA LEGRIS Poetry printed by permission of the author. LYN LIFSHIN Poetry printed by permission of the author. MARCIA LIPSON Poetry printed by permission of the author. JEFF MANN Poetry printed by permission of the author. ELISE M. MCCLELLAN Poetry printed by permission of the author. SEYMOUR MAYNE "Milk" from *Children of Abel* (Mosaic Press). Poetry printed by permission of the author. WESLEY MCNAIR "The Fat Enter Heaven" from *Poetry* and *The Town of No* (David R. Godine, 1989). Poetry printed by permission of the author. SANDRA MCPHERSON "Food" from *Bakunin.* Poetry printed by permission of the author. SHEILA MEADS Prose printed by permission of the author. SCOTT MINAR Poetry printed by permission of the author. FELICIA MITCHELL "Eggs" from *The Cloverdale Review of Criticism and Poetry.* Poetry printed by permission of the author. HAYLEY R. MITCHELL "Suzie gets a colander" from *Blank Gun Silencer # 7.* Poetry printed by permission of the author. PATRICIA MONAGHAN Poetry printed by permission of the author. SUSAN MUSGRAVE "Love Wasn't Always" from *Forcing the Narcissus* (McClelland & Stewart). Poetry printed by permission of the author. BPNICHOL "The Mouth" and "The Tonsils" from *Selected Organs* (Black Moss Press) and *An H in the Heart* (McClelland & Stewart). Poetry printed by permission of Ellie Nichol. ALDEN NOWLAN "And He Wept Aloud, So That the Egyptians Heard It" from *An Exchange of Gifts* (Irwin Publishing). Poetry printed by permission of Stoddart Publishing Company. DAVID OATES Prose printed by permission of the author. DIANA O'HEHIR "Apple" from *Home Free* (Atheneum). Poetry printed by permission of the author. MICHAEL ONDAATJE "The Cinnamon Peeler" from *The Cinnamon Peeler* (McClelland & Stewart) and (Alfred A. Knopf Inc.). Poetry reprinted